MEREDITH KLEYKAMP, JEFFREY B. WENGER,
ELIZABETH HASTINGS ROER, MATTHEW KUBASAK,
TRAVIS HUBBLE, LAUREN SKRABALA

Federal Programs to Assist Military-to-Civilian Employment Transitions

Limited Scrutiny and Substantial Investment in Education Programs

For more information on this publication, visit **www.rand.org/t/RRA1363-12**.

About RAND

RAND is a research organization that develops solutions to public policy challenges to help make communities throughout the world safer and more secure, healthier and more prosperous. RAND is nonprofit, nonpartisan, and committed to the public interest. To learn more about RAND, visit www.rand.org.

Research Integrity

Our mission to help improve policy and decisionmaking through research and analysis is enabled through our core values of quality and objectivity and our unwavering commitment to the highest level of integrity and ethical behavior. To help ensure our research and analysis are rigorous, objective, and nonpartisan, we subject our research publications to a robust and exacting quality-assurance process; avoid both the appearance and reality of financial and other conflicts of interest through staff training, project screening, and a policy of mandatory disclosure; and pursue transparency in our research engagements through our commitment to the open publication of our research findings and recommendations, disclosure of the source of funding of published research, and policies to ensure intellectual independence. For more information, visit www.rand.org/about/research-integrity.

RAND's publications do not necessarily reflect the opinions of its research clients and sponsors.

Published by the RAND Corporation, Santa Monica, Calif.
© 2024 RAND Corporation
RAND® is a registered trademark.

Library of Congress Cataloging-in-Publication Data is available for this publication.
ISBN: 978-1-9774-1343-7

Cover Photo: Gorodenkoff/Adobe Stock.

About This Report

Service members make many transitions throughout their careers—from location to location, from military job to military job, and, eventually, to civilian life. For many service members, the military-to-civilian transition is the most fraught, requiring such important decisions as where to live and how to earn a living. As they prepare to enter the civilian labor market, transitioning service members and veterans can benefit from job-search support and opportunities to apply the skills that they developed during their time in the military. For some, the transition period is an ideal time to pursue additional training or education. The spouses of service members and veterans, who might have sacrificed career opportunities to the demands of military service, can also benefit from employment support.

To meet these diverse needs, the federal government funds a variety of programs to support military-to-civilian employment transitions. However, relatively little information is available about how these programs allocate their budgets and whether they effectively aid skilled veterans in finding civilian employment at a family-sustaining wage, despite these programs being funded by billions of dollars. Starting with a set of 45 programs identified by the U.S. Government Accountability Office as providing employment support for service members, veterans, and dependents, we have explored which programs consume outsized levels of funding relative to the number of participants they serve. We also identify gaps in the evaluation research, shortfalls in available budget and participation data, and opportunities to improve the return on federal investment and better meet the needs of those who depend on these programs as they reintegrate into civilian life.

Policymakers, those who design and implement programming, nonprofits that help in postseparation re-employment, and funders (including foundations and private philanthropies) that provide resources to the nonprofit sector all benefit from a clear and accurate understanding of the landscape in which they operate. This report complements another RAND report on nonprofit-sector programs that support transitioning service members, *Increasing Sustainability of Veteran-Serving Employment-Focused Nonprofits: Findings from a Mixed-Methods Study* (Kleykamp et al., forthcoming). Together, these reports provide a fuller picture of the resources available to this population, highlighting opportunities for closer collaboration and helping funders identify and fill unmet employment transition needs.

The RAND Epstein Family Veterans Policy Research Institute

The RAND Epstein Family Veterans Policy Research Institute is dedicated to conducting innovative, evidence-based research and analysis to improve the lives of those who have served in the U.S. military. Building on decades of interdisciplinary expertise at RAND, the institute prioritizes creative, equitable, and inclusive solutions and interventions that meet the needs of diverse veteran populations while engaging and empowering those who support them. For more information about the RAND Epstein Family Veterans Policy Research

Institute, visit veterans.rand.org. Questions about this report or about the RAND Epstein Family Veterans Policy Research Institute should be directed to veteranspolicy@rand.org.

Funding

Funding for this publication was made possible by a generous gift from Daniel J. Epstein through the Epstein Family Foundation, which established the RAND Epstein Family Veterans Policy Research Institute in 2021.

This research was funded through additional support from The Heinz Endowments, which seeks to help southwestern Pennsylvania thrive as a whole and just community and, through that work, to model solutions to major national and global challenges.

Acknowledgments

We thank Stephen Dalzell from RAND and Jason Dempsey from Columbia University for their helpful feedback that greatly improved this report. We also thank Benjamin Master for overseeing the quality assurance process for this report. We offer special thanks to Carrie Farmer and Rajeev Ramchand of the Veterans Policy Research Institute for developing this line of inquiry and supporting the research. We would also like to thank The Heinz Endowments for its generous support.

Summary

The particulars of transitioning from military life to civilian life are different for every veteran. Success in translating the skills acquired during military service to the civilian labor market varies by military occupation and other variables, such as whether the service member was deployed, is married, has children, or spent a few or many years in service. Transition aids, such as training, education, career advice, and job support, can boost veterans' job prospects and help them find or develop fulfilling careers in civilian life. The U.S. government offers a transition support program to facilitate almost every conceivable military-to-civilian transition path. However, as prior RAND research has shown, many veterans still feel that they are unable to leverage their military skills in their civilian jobs (see Wenger, Pint, et al., 2017).

The federal government spends more than $13 billion each year on these transition programs (see Table B.1 in Appendix B). However, there has been little analysis of how this funding is apportioned, how programs use their funding, where there is potential overlap between programs, and how effective these programs are. In response to a request from Congress, the U.S. Government Accountability Office (GAO) assessed the federally funded programs that helped transitioning service members, veterans, and their families acquire skills and education to prepare them for civilian employment (GAO, 2019a; GAO, 2020). GAO catalogued 45 such programs that are overseen by 11 federal agencies, including the U.S. Department of Defense (DoD), U.S. Department of Veterans Affairs (VA), and U.S. Department of Labor (DOL). GAO found a great deal of overlap in the activities and goals of the 45 programs, as well as variation in their budgets and the extent to which the agencies evaluated the effectiveness of their programs. GAO also noted that more than 97 percent of federal expenditures were allocated to educational assistance across the 45 programs. Although further education is important for many veterans, most veterans enter the civilian workforce directly and might benefit from more employment-focused support.

To update and extend GAO's analysis and to ultimately help improve military-to-civilian transition outcomes for U.S. veterans, we seek to map the current landscape of employment-focused transition programs. We rely heavily on publicly available data, much of which comes from GAO reports; part of this reliance is because GAO reports are the only source of systematic data and programmatic information. In this study, we investigate costs of transition programs, identify the programs that are the most expensive, and examine the programs' effects on the transition landscape. We also explore the policy dynamics that have enabled programs to continue operating even though they have not published detailed data on the populations they serve, how they allocate their budgets, and how they track their performance.

How the Study Was Conducted

To facilitate this analysis, we review the literature on employment transition programs, assess budgetary and policy documents, and compile a comprehensive review of how federal transition programs function. In this report, we also seek to understand whom and how many people the programs serve and what evidence is available to indicate how the programs perform.

We find that little has changed since 2022, when GAO conducted its last study: The same 45 programs remain active, and, except for a few pilot programs, there have been no additions to the employment transition landscape. Thus, we have grouped, according to budget size, the same 45 programs that GAO originally identified. This allows the programs to be divided into the following four categories:

1. **"Big Four" budgetary programs**: the Post-9/11 GI Bill (PGIB), Veteran Readiness and Employment, DoD's Tuition Assistance Program, and Survivors' and Dependents' Educational Assistance
2. **second-tier programs**: the Montgomery GI Bill and Jobs for Veterans State Grants
3. **third-tier program**: DoD's Transition Assistance Program (TAP)
4. **small programs**: an assortment of additional programs with significantly smaller budgets that serve significantly smaller target populations than the other three categories of programs.

Key Findings

Most Employment Transition Programs Are Actually Focused on Education

Overall, we find that very few programs focus on military-to-civilian employment transitions. Specifically, little support is dedicated to helping service members and veterans translate their military skills to the civilian labor market. There is also limited assistance for finding civilian apprenticeships or jobs, and few resources are available for connecting them with civilian employers. In fact, nearly all the money for *career assistance programs*, as defined by GAO, is spent on upskilling, retraining, or education programs. With limited exceptions, such programs can take many months or years to complete. These programs offer valuable opportunities to enhance veterans' knowledge, skills, and employment opportunities. Dedicating significant portions of the transition budget is also unsurprising because of the high and growing costs of college. However, many veterans want or need to move directly into employment. Programs that support immediate employment transitions beyond the mandatory TAP are surprisingly limited.

There Is Limited Evidence That Federally Funded Employment Transition Programs Are Effective

There is virtually no evidence that any of the programs we examine have had a direct effect on transition outcomes. In some cases, the evidence is counterintuitive; for example, the large, interagency TAP, which is overseen by DoD, is associated with lower wages for program participants. Similarly, the PGIB has resulted in modest increases in education but limited increases in earnings and, in some cases, has even resulted in negative returns on investment in schooling. Other programs have no reported data, evaluation plans, resources, or outcome measures. Perhaps as a result, there have been few evaluations of program effectiveness.

Transition Programs Face Limited Oversight and Budgetary Scrutiny

The largest budgetary program, the PGIB, provides little information on participation and outcomes, i.e., how many service members and veterans use it and whether they graduate from their programs. Overall, we find that oversight is weak across all 45 programs. This finding could be because oversight of these programs is fragmented; numerous congressional committees are responsible for overseeing portions of some programs, and various federal agencies are involved in operating these programs.

One outcome of this oversight challenge is that program redundancies are common. This is especially true for education programs that provide general counseling and services.

There Are Opportunities to Address Redundancies in Transition Programs and Services

We find numerous redundancies in available transition programs and services. There are many specific occupational skill-focused training programs that serve relatively limited numbers of participants. There are opportunities to consolidate multiple programs that provide on-the-job training in specific skill sets to reduce overhead costs, avoid duplication of effort, and improve outreach. The involvement of multiple federal agencies can make this consolidation challenging, so this is an area in need of more research. In general, a large number of transition programs serve a small population, and, without sufficient evaluation of the return on investment from these programs, it is difficult to identify which specific programs could be consolidated or discontinued to make resources available to others.

Recommendations

There is a great deal of inconsistency in how budgets are reported across the transition-assistance programs, even the large ones, and we encounter few robust evaluations of their outcomes in the employment transition landscape. Because the federal government spends an estimated $13 billion annually on education, training, and other aspects of military-to-civilian employment transitions, it is critical that the agencies that receive these funds are held accountable for consistently reporting how their program budgets are allocated and whom they have served. One challenge we faced is locating reliable, updated budget numbers; this could be a result of shortfalls in oversight and variations in reporting requirements.

The most notable gap is the paucity of program evaluations. Although there have been congressionally mandated assessments of some programs, much of the information we find on program effectiveness comes from small-scale or otherwise limited studies.

Our study suggests that there is a deep need to improve the military-to-civilian transition program landscape. The following recommendations can help policymakers identify opportunities to reduce spending on redundant or ineffective programs and to better address the needs of transitioning service members, veterans, and their families.

- **Conduct an independent evaluation of the largest programs to reduce inefficiencies and improve performance.** Most federal funding for employment transitions goes to programs that exclusively or primarily support educational opportunities. Many questions about the efficiency and effectiveness of these programs could be answered by an independent evaluation of the largest programs conducted by an agency that is empowered to access detailed budget information and performance evaluation results. For example, this evaluation might answer the research question: To what extent are federal funds going toward education at the *expense* of successful employment transitions?
- **Refocus military-to-civilian transition support on employment.** This study identifies ways to use federal funding to better help service members and veterans switch to civilian jobs. One option is to invest in programs that help them transition quickly, especially those programs offering personalized support. For example, TAP leadership might consider renewing the program's focus on helping transitioning service members find jobs that align with their skills, as well as providing continuing support post-separation. Finally, there might be opportunities for DoD to outsource career counseling through vouchers for the services of local private-sector professionals. Such "boots-on-the-ground" personnel might be better positioned than federally employed career counselors to help veterans transition to the civilian labor market in their local area. They might also be able to provide long-term support.
- **Mandate consistent and routine budget reporting for all programs that support military-to-civilian transitions.** There is a need for policymaker intervention to require agencies to standardize their budget and performance reporting—a mandate that should not be limited to programs that support employment transitions. In its 2020 report, GAO relied on self-reported budgetary data from program representatives, which leads to questions about the completeness and accuracy of this information. As we have attempted to update those findings, we often find outdated and conflicting budgetary information, even for large programs.
- **Identify opportunities to streamline the employment transition landscape and improve oversight.** Although the smallest programs have limited budgets, they collectively receive millions of dollars in federal funding. Individually, these programs serve small numbers of beneficiaries, and there is little information about their performance.

Excess programs can complicate the benefit landscape for veterans who already need to navigate an enormous number of resources. Increased oversight, combined with a full-scale study of these small, federally funded employment transition programs, would provide the necessary evidence for decisions about which programs should be shuttered or combined with existing programs.

Contents

Figures and Tables

Figures

Tables

CHAPTER 1

The Federal Military-to-Civilian Budget Landscape

Service members make many transitions throughout their careers—from location to location, from military job to military job, and, eventually, to civilian life. For many service members, the military-to-civilian transition is the most fraught, requiring such important decisions as where to live and how to earn a living. As transitioning service members and veterans prepare to enter the civilian labor market, they can benefit from opportunities to apply the skills that they developed over their time in the military—whether they served for a few years or many years—and to pursue a civilian career that both is rewarding and aligns with their skills and interests.

The military-to-civilian transition is unique for every veteran. An officer's transition to a civilian career might look very different from that of someone in the enlisted ranks. The skill sets and experiences of a Marine Corps infantryman or an Air Force maintenance specialist differ significantly from those of a Navy hospital corpsman or an Army combat medic. The response to the question of what constitutes a "good" civilian transition should be couched in terms of transition *from what* and *to what*.

Not every service member who is seeking civilian employment will transition directly from the armed forces to the labor market. Some might pursue an apprenticeship, attend a trade or technical school, enroll in a two- or four-year college, or even start their own businesses. For each of these possible postservice futures, the U.S. government offers a transition-support program to facilitate it. However, the *existence* of a program tells us very little about how often it is used, how effective it is, or whether it is a good investment. This last point is the primary focus of this research.

In response to a request from Congress, the U.S. Government Accountability Office (GAO) assessed the federally funded programs that help transitioning service members, veterans, and their families acquire skills and education to prepare them for civilian employment (GAO, 2019a; GAO, 2020). GAO catalogued 45 programs overseen by 11 federal agencies, including the U.S. Department of Defense (DoD), U.S. Department of Veterans Affairs (VA), and U.S. Department of Labor (DOL), and found a great deal of overlap in these programs' activities and goals. GAO's analysis also examined program budgets and the extent to which the programs had been evaluated on their effectiveness. Our analysis finds that little has changed since the time of the GAO study: The same 45 programs remain active, and, with the exception of a few pilot programs, there have been no new additions to the employment transition landscape. Thus, we have grouped these 45 programs by the size of their budgets into four categories—"Big Four" budgetary programs; second-tier programs; third-tier program; and small programs—which we explain further below.

Research Approach

To map the current landscape of employment-focused transition programs, we investigate their costs, identify the programs that are the most expensive, and examine the programs' effects on the transition landscape. We also explore the policy dynamics that have enabled programs to continue operating even though they have not published detailed data on the populations they serve, how they allocate their budgets, and how they track their performance.

In the course of our analyses, we look at who was making the transition from military to civilian life and which resources were available to them, their spouses, and their children. Finally, we examine eligibility for benefits among members of the National Guard and reserves, as well as those who serve in other armed forces, such as the Coast Guard.

Figure 1.1 tracks patterns in federal spending on programs to support military-to-civilian employment transitions since 1962.

FIGURE 1.1

Federal Expenditures on Education, Training, and Rehabilitation for Transitioning Service Members and Veterans, 1962–2021

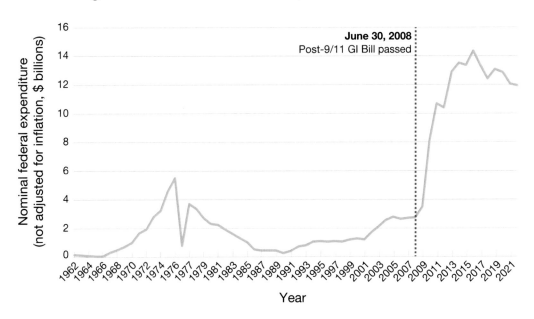

SOURCE: Features data from White House, Office of Management and Budget, undated, Table 9.9.

The Budgetary Big Four

GAO identified 45 federal government programs that provide transition assistance to service members and their families. Four of these programs—and one, in particular—command an outsized share of expenditures. The Post-9/11 GI Bill (PGIB), Veteran Readiness and Employment (VR&E),[1] DoD's Tuition Assistance Program, and the Survivors' and Dependents' Educational Assistance (DEA) collectively account for 94 percent of the $14.3 billion that the federal government spent on military-to-civilian transition assistance in 2017 (GAO, 2020). Figure 1.2 shows the non-inflation-adjusted federal spending for each of these programs in fiscal year (FY) 2022 in billions of U.S. dollars.

Three of these four programs are dedicated to supporting educational advancement. PGIB reimburses tuition and provides a stipend to veterans who served in the military since September 11, 2001, while they pursue education or training; DEA provides a stipend to support the education of dependents of veterans who have a disability rating of 100 percent; and DoD's Tuition Assistance Program reimburses the cost of the courses that active-duty service members take while they are off duty. The remaining program, VR&E, offers a suite of career assistance and medical rehabilitation services to disabled veterans. However, more

FIGURE 1.2

Federal Expenditures on the Budgetary Big Four Programs, FY 2022

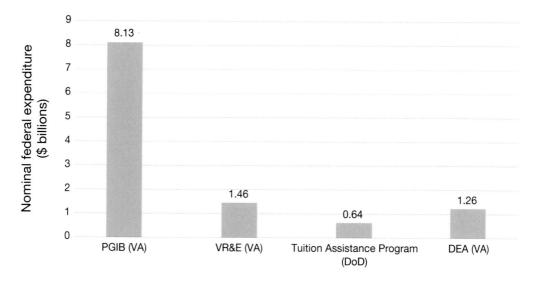

SOURCES: Features data on the PGIB, VR&E, and DEA from Veterans Benefits Administration (VBA), 2023a, pp. 157, 214, 11; and data on DoD's Tuition Assistance Program from Kamarck, 2023, p. 6, Table 2.

NOTE: The agency responsible for each program is in parentheses. Budget amounts for DoD's Tuition Assistance Program represent total funding for voluntary education programs administered by the military services. Service budget documentation does not consistently break out Tuition Assistance Program funding as a separate line item.

---

[1] This program was previously known as Vocational Rehabilitation and Employment.

than 95 percent of that program's expenditures are for educational assistance, which includes tuition reimbursement and a stipend. Educational assistance is the overall budgetary focus for all transition-assistance programs, not only for the Big Four. More than 97 percent of federal expenditures were allocated to educational assistance across the 45 programs that GAO identified.

We have followed GAO's lead in including all programs that provide career assistance to service members and their families in our analyses. Some, such as DoD's Tuition Assistance Program, provide civilian educational opportunities to service members before they leave the military. Others, such as the PGIB and its predecessor, the Montgomery GI Bill (MGIB), support the pursuit of education either during or after military service. We consider that all these programs are forms of career assistance for the simple reason that civilian education can facilitate transitions to the civilian labor market, whether that education is pursued during or after military service. Some programs, such as DEA and, in some cases, the PGIB, support service members' families because families often sacrifice employment opportunities to the demands of the service member's military career and veterans might continue to depend on family members after leaving the military. By providing educational opportunities to the dependents of 100-percent disabled veterans, DEA facilitates the livelihood of both veterans and their families.

In addition to serving both military members and their dependents, the programs identified as transition programs often serve other purposes. The PGIB enhances postservice training and education but also serves as a recruiting and retention tool. Similarly, Military OneSource is a family-support program, not merely a transition program, and offers family members information and assistance in finding jobs while their related military members are serving and as they transition. Although most programs have multiple purposes, those examined in this report serve the transition needs of military members and their families.

Education-focused transition programs that target current service members can both ease military-to-civilian transitions and provide direct benefits to the armed forces in the form of improved job performance or higher retention rates (Mehay and Pema, 2008); and some, such as DoD's Tuition Assistance Program and the PGIB, require extended service commitments. Educational benefits can also serve as a recruitment tool. However, the research supporting these claims is limited. A RAND study by Wenger, Miller, et al. (2017) showed that the PGIB had a small positive effect on recruiting that was accompanied by an even smaller decline in retention. The motivation for these educational programs is sometimes expressed in terms of a moral obligation to reward sacrifice on the part of both service members and their families rather than as a way to achieve a specific outcome. The multiple purposes of these educational assistance programs can make it difficult to evaluate their effectiveness. Perhaps because of this challenge, the few evaluations that have been conducted have focused almost exclusively on the quality of the programs, particularly the risks of potentially predatory for-profit educational institutions, rather than their effects on earnings, recruitment, or retention.

Another gap in the research is whether tuition assistance and other educational benefits privilege certain groups of service members and veterans—those with particular military jobs, those with access to computers and the internet, or those who have the time and energy to engage in additional coursework. A report by Wenger and Ward (2022) found that women and African Americans were more likely to use DoD tuition assistance and more likely to earn a college degree than other service members and veterans.

The Second-Tier Programs

Recruiting challenges across the active and reserve components in 1985 motivated Congress to replace the Post-Vietnam Veterans' Educational Assistance Program with the more generous MGIB for service members who meet active-duty service requirements, as well as at a lower benefit level for those who do not meet those requirements but extend their commitments in the Selected Reserve. The MGIB provides monthly payments for up to 36 months to assist with tuition and fees, supplies, books, and equipment; some participants receive additional assistance under complementary programs designed to facilitate targeted recruiting efforts. MGIB assistance can be used for a wide variety of approved postsecondary education or training programs, including licensing exams, tutoring, apprenticeships, and on-the-job training. Under the MGIB, active-duty service members must elect to have their first year of military pay reduced by $100 per month to contribute to the program; then, they are eligible to receive monthly benefits after a qualifying period of active-duty service (typically three years) in either the active or reserve component or after they separate from the military under honorable conditions.

Evaluations of the MGIB have found that it modestly increased the probability that veterans enrolled in postsecondary education but also increased the likelihood that service members separated from the military. In general, the MGIB is less generous than the PGIB. The MGIB is being phased out and scheduled to stop accepting new participants in FY 2031.

Jobs for Veterans State Grants (JVSG) funds veteran employment support services at state workforce agencies. The program entitles veterans and eligible surviving spouses to priority access, which is termed *priority of service*, to DOL-funded employment and training programs. Veterans, transitioning service members, and spouses who face significant barriers to employment receive additional priority. States receive grant funding in proportion to their share of unemployed veterans. Employment support is provided to veterans through dedicated staff at state American Job Centers, at which many other forms of DOL-funded employment assistance are offered to the general population. The program was created by the Jobs for Veterans Act (Pub. L. 107-288, 2002) by reorganizing several existing employment programs for veterans, devolving service provision to the state level, and improving federal oversight of grant spending.

Program analysis in Thompson et al. (2015) found that JVSG veterans had better employment outcomes than non-JVSG veterans and nonveterans who used American Job Center services. However, their analysis did not control for possible selection bias and could not distinguish between program effects and preexisting differences among study populations.

Figure 1.3 shows the non-inflation-adjusted federal spending in millions of U.S. dollars for both second-tier programs. MGIB data, which are separated by the active-duty and Selected Reserve components, are from FY 2022, whereas JVSG data are from FY 2017, which are the most recent available.

The Third-Tier Program

The 1990s saw a significant drawdown of U.S. military forces—a result of the changing geopolitical climate, including the end of the Cold War, as well as budget constraints and shifting public opinion about the military's role in U.S. foreign policy. The drawdown pushed a large number of veterans into the civilian labor market, resulting in high unemployment rates for this population. DoD launched the Transition Assistance Program (TAP) in 1991 to better prepare transitioning service members for civilian life, but early evaluations found that it was poorly designed and implemented, and that the program had virtually no infrastructure to identify which service members were likely to leave the military, which services would be helpful, and how to deliver those services.

The 1996 Congressional Commission on Servicemembers and Veterans Transition Assistance found that the TAP and other existing transition-assistance programs for military personnel and veterans were inadequate and required significant improvements. The com-

FIGURE 1.3

Federal Expenditures on the Second-Tier Programs, 2017 and 2022

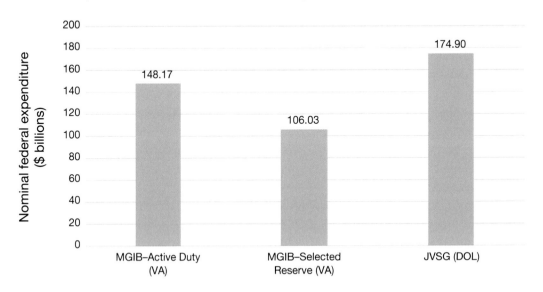

SOURCES: Features FY 2022 data on the MGIB from VBA, 2023a, p. 156; and FY 2017 data on JVSG from GAO, 2020, p. 24, Table 6.
NOTE: The agency responsible for each program is in parentheses. The MGIB is being phased out and will no longer accept new enrollees after September 30, 2030.

mission's report, released in 1999, recommended that DoD and VA work together to create a comprehensive transition-assistance program that included job training, education, and counseling services. Since then, GAO has written several reports that are critical of the envisioned TAP, highlighting the need for enhanced services, outreach to transitioning service members, coordination among command leadership and service providers, reporting on program participation, and oversight.

The VOW (Veterans Opportunity to Work) to Hire Heroes Act of 2011 (Pub. L. 112-56, Title II, 2011) made several changes to the TAP to better support transitioning service members and veterans. These changes included mandatory participation, expanded services, personalized assistance, preseparation counseling, and follow-up services.

One comprehensive evaluation of the TAP, which was sponsored by DOL's Chief Evaluation Office, concluded that U.S. Army participants found civilian work more quickly than nonparticipants, remained employed longer, and had lower unemployment rates at 12 months after military separation—although not at six months after separation (O'Conner, Schoeneberger, and Clark, 2023). TAP participants, on average, earned less than their peers who had not participated in the program, although starting the TAP earlier in the transition process and participating in sessions on VA benefits and financial planning appeared to counteract this effect to some extent (O'Conner, Schoeneberger, and Clark, 2023). Overall, evidence on the performance of the TAP is limited by self-selection effects. The newest design features of the TAP facilitate a good quasi-experimental research design, and DoD's data merging with the U.S. Census Bureau will allow researchers to link military experience to civilian labor market outcomes.[2]

The Small Programs

The vast majority of federal funding for service members' military-to-civilian employment transitions goes to the five programs already discussed: PGIB education benefits, VR&E, DoD's Tuition Assistance Program, DEA for dependents, and the TAP. However, there are many other programs that address more-specialized needs, such as apprenticeship and job-matching programs, that can even enhance the effects of the largest employment-transition support programs. We note that some of the best ideas in transition assistance are happening at a smaller scale. Calls to shutter such programs should be accompanied by plans to replicate those good ideas at scale in other programs. Despite such insights from various small

---

[2] This initiative of the Office of Economic and Manpower Analysis, housed at the United States Military Academy at West Point, will link data from DoD's Defense Manpower Data Center with data from the U.S. Census Bureau's Longitudinal Employer-Household Dynamics program, which collects federal and state employment statistics, and the National Directory of New Hires, a federal reporting system for personal data on employed Americans and those receiving unemployment benefits (see O'Conner, Schoeneberger, and Clark [2023] for more details).

programs, we find a great deal overlap both among these small programs and with the larger federal programs that they often supplement.

To facilitate our review of these myriad small programs, we categorize them according to the following four primary goals but acknowledge that most programs are not single-faceted:

- **general education and employment counseling programs**, which help transitioning service members and veterans build life plans and assess their education and employment needs and preferences
- **education-focused programs** that provide funding, counseling, and accreditation services
- **employment-focused programs** that help transitioning service members and veterans develop employment skills, assist with job searches and on-the-job employer interactions, and connect program participants with jobs or apprenticeships
- **transition programs for nonveterans and general benefit support programs**, which support the family members of transitioning service members and veterans or help veterans access benefits that are not directly related to education or employment.

Our review of these small programs is limited to a high-level assessment of their goals, activities, and areas of redundancy and overlap. Although individual program budgets might be small, they collectively receive millions of dollars in federal funding. Therefore, there would be a benefit to pursuing a dedicated full-scale analysis of small-program uptake and effectiveness.

In Figure 1.4, we provide a visualization of all the programs discussed in the report showing the beneficiary type (e.g., veteran, spouse, child) and the transition phase when the benefits are available.

Finally, throughout this report, we note that there is a lack of data and performance assessments for most of these transition programs. We address this topic as part of our conclusions, but it is important to mention here that most programs do not have platforms designed for performance tracking. For example, one major DOL assessment of the TAP used Army data on soldiers who enrolled in and completed the TAP (see O'Conner, Schoeneberger, and Clark, 2023). The researchers then matched participants with the National Directory of New Hires to see when those who did and did not complete the TAP curriculum became employed. Then, they combined those results with the Longitudinal Employer Household Database to examine longer-term employment outcomes. Thus, the study required researchers to combine multiple datasets that needed to be analyzed in secure facilities because they contained participants' personally identifiable information.

We also note that, in many cases, we simply do not know much about the population that did not receive benefits. It might be that there is considerable positive program participation selection (i.e., those who are most aware of the program are proactive in receiving benefits, and the untreated population is faring poorly), or this might not be the case. To address this evidence gap, it is critical for program evaluators to survey a nonparticipating comparison group, and all surveys would be ideally administered at regular intervals.

FIGURE 1.4
Roadmap to Federal Transition Programs: Beneficiaries and Benefit Timing

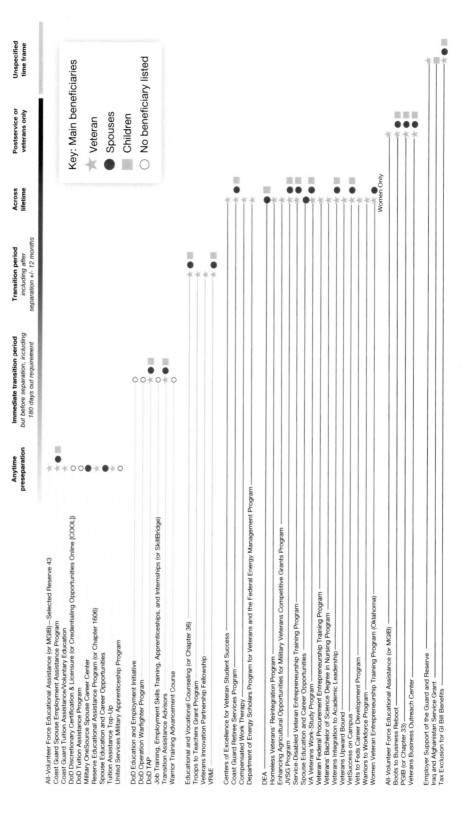

In pursuing such studies, researchers would have to develop meaningful outcome measures driven by program goals. Education-focused program evaluations would need to answer such basic questions as whether individual veterans graduated or completed degree requirements, whether they incurred debt, and whether they found a job in a field related to their degree. For employment-focused programs, it would be important to evaluate, at a minimum, how long it took to find work, measures of job satisfaction, job tenure, pay, and benefits. Evaluations of entrepreneurship programs should focus on rates of business success and failure, earnings, profits, hours of work, and health insurance access. Again, survey design and outcome measures would be dependent on the goals of the program. Because of the expense of these programs, the costs of evaluations and related analyses are likely negligible, and there is the potential to recoup these costs through improved program performance or enhanced efficiency.

Better research designs, such as the random controlled trials used in evaluations of Social Security Disability Insurance, Temporary Assistance for Needy Families, Workforce Innovation and Opportunity Act initiatives, and other federal programs, could be implemented for the transition programs discussed in this report. However, because of the difficulty of random assignment for some programs, including the TAP and the PGIB, this approach might not be feasible. Finally, we note that, in some cases, carefully conducted randomized controlled trials have provided mixed evidence of success. See Barnow and Smith (2023) for a review of federal employment and training program evaluation methods.

Organization of This Report

The remainder of this report reviews the history of each of these transition-assistance programs and the policies that led to their establishment, enhancement, and current implementation; the goals of the respective programs and the populations they target; and key findings from past evaluations of their effectiveness. Chapter 2 examines the budgetary Big Four programs: the PGIB, VR&E, DoD's Tuition Assistance Program, and DEA. Chapter 3 looks at the two second-tier programs: the MGIB and JVSG. Chapter 4 focuses on the third-tier program, the TAP, and Chapter 5 highlights a selection of smaller programs. Chapter 6 provides details on our analysis and findings, in which we review the most-current evidence for each of the programs, identify their funding and activities, and assess any evaluations of their effectiveness. Chapter 7 presents our conclusions and recommendations. Two appendixes accompany this report: Appendix A provides a detailed legislative history of the 45 transition programs, and Appendix B provides updated budget information for any programs that made such figures available.

CHAPTER 2

The Budgetary Big Four: PGIB, VR&E, DoD's Tuition Assistance Program, and DEA

Benefits for service members, veterans, and, in some cases, their families through the PGIB, VR&E, DoD's Tuition Assistance Program, and DEA receive an outsized share of federal funding dedicated to military-to-civilian transition assistance. With the exception of VR&E, these programs focus on helping beneficiaries advance their education. In this chapter and subsequent ones, we begin with a brief history of each program, identify the populations it targets, and outline the program's goals. We conclude each program's section by characterizing the evaluation literature, highlighting key findings about program effectiveness, and assessing the strength of the evidence supporting these findings.

The Post-9/11 GI Bill (PGIB)

History and Policy Changes

Education benefits for veterans date back to 1944, when eligible World War II veterans received one year of full-time training plus a period equal to their time in service, up to 48 months. The stated purpose was "to provide federal government aid for the readjustment in civilian life of returning World War II veterans" (Pub. L. 78-346, 1944).[1] In 1952, benefits were extended to Korean War veterans but limited to 36 months (Pub. L. 82-550, 1952). Education benefits were extended to all veterans in 1966. Congress gave multiple reasons for this expansion in the Veterans Readjustment Benefits Act of 1966, including (1) enhancing military recruitment, (2) providing the benefits of a higher education to young people who might not otherwise be able to afford it, and (3) providing vocational training and restoring educational opportunities lost to active-duty military service (Pub. L. 89-358, 1966). Almost

---

[1] Eligibility was limited to those "whose education or training was impeded, delayed, interrupted, or interfered with by reason of his entrance into the service," but this was deemed true for any service members who were up to 25 years old when they entered the service (Pub. L. 78-346, Title II, Part VIII, 1944, p. 288).

two decades later, the MGIB changed the landscape of military-to-civilian transitions again (Pub. L. 98-525, Sections 701–709, 1985), which we discuss in Chapter 3.[2]

The PGIB, which went into effect on August 1, 2009, triggered a major shift in veteran education benefits (Pub. L. 110-252, Title V, 2008). The PGIB offered an alternative to the MGIB that did not require service members to make payments during their military careers and substantially increased available education benefits.[3] This change in benefits provided a significant boost in the incentives to enroll in postsecondary education and training. Consequently, the PGIB came with increased costs as well: VA spent roughly $2 billion on MGIB benefits in 2008, whereas in 2017, it spent more than $11 billion on PGIB benefits. A 2021 Congressional Research Service assessment found that the PGIB "has represented more than 70% of total GI Bill participation and more than 80% of spending in each year since FY2013. In FY2022, the program is estimated to benefit over 600,000 individuals and expend almost $10 billion" (Dortch, 2021a, p. 1).

The PGIB provides education and training benefits to qualifying veterans—and their family members, in certain circumstances—for approved programs. Benefits can include reimbursement for tuition and fees, licensing and certification test fees, and tutorial fees, as well as a housing allowance, relocation assistance, and a stipend for books and supplies (Dortch, 2021a). To be eligible, service members must typically have served a minimum of 90 days on qualifying active duty after September 10, 2001, and those who use the benefits after separating from active duty need to have separated from the military under honorable conditions (VBA, 2024).[4] Under some circumstances, PGIB benefits can be transferred to family members (U.S. Code, Title 38, Chapter 33, Section 3319).

The duration of assistance depends on several factors, including active-duty status, length of qualifying active-duty service, and the characteristics of the educational pursuit. The duration of benefits aligns with the qualifying period of service; for example, a service member with 18 months of qualifying active-duty service is eligible for 18 months of educational assistance, while a service member with 36 months or more receives the maximum entitlement of 36 months of benefits. In terms of the monetary value of these benefits, the maximum tuition payment for a public institution of higher learning is the in-state rate plus fees; for a private institution, it is the lesser of the actual tuition and a national private school maximum reimbursement rate that is tied to the national average cost for public education. Under the Yellow Ribbon program, if a private institution's tuition and fees exceed the reimbursement cap, the

---

[2] For a more exhaustive discussion of the history of military educational benefits, see Smole and Loane (2008).

[3] According to the Congressional Research Service, "Post-9/11 GI Bill–eligible individuals with a single qualifying active duty service period must make an *irrevocable* election to give up benefits under one of the applicable programs to receive benefits under the Post-9/11 GI Bill" (Dortch, 2021a, p. 6).

[4] A veteran qualifies after 30 continuous days if released from active-duty service because of a service-connected disability, and there is no time-served requirement if the veteran received a Purple Heart. Note that this is more restrictive than the Survivors' and Dependents' Education Assistance program, which requires a discharge other than dishonorable.

institution can voluntarily enter into an agreement with VA to match an equal percentage of some portion of the remaining tuition and fees (U.S. Code, Title 38, Chapter 33, Section 3317). Public institutions receiving VA tuition payments (from the PGIB, MGIB, DEA, or VR&E) must also charge in-resident tuition rates to qualifying beneficiaries.[5] Unlike the MGIB, the PGIB requires that the VA pay tuition and fees directly to the institution of higher learning. Qualifying beneficiaries directly receive a stipend for books and supplies of up to $1,000 per academic year, as well as a housing allowance equivalent to the military's Basic Allowance for Housing for service members with a rank of E-5 with dependents, which varies by location (U.S. Code, Title 38, Chapter 33, Section 3313). In 2023, this amount could reach as high as $4,644 per month. For courses taken online or at a foreign school, the housing allowance was $1,054.50 in 2023, which is equal to half of the national average for housing costs (VA, 2024a).

The following policy changes significantly changed how the PGIB has been administered since its inception.

- In 2009, benefits were extended to spouses and children of service members who died in the line of duty or from a service-connected disability while a member of the Selected Reserve; benefits were also extended to reservists and National Guard members who are called to active duty for training or operations (Pub. L. 111-32, Section 1002, 2009).
- In 2010, the tuition reimbursement cap for private institutions was fixed at $17,500, adjusted annually based on an index of the average increase in the cost of undergraduate tuition (Pub. L. 111-377, 2011).
- In 2014, schools were permitted to receive PGIB payments only if they offered in-state tuition rates to qualifying beneficiaries (Pub. L. 113-146, Section 702, 2014).
- In 2015, veterans were prohibited from receiving unemployment compensation and PGIB benefits concurrently (Pub. L. 114-92, Section 560, 2015).
- In 2017, the "Forever GI Bill" eliminated the 15-year time limit on the use of benefits by service members who were discharged after January 1, 2013, as well as expanded eligibility and modified benefit amounts (Pub. L. 115-48, 2017). Service members who were discharged before January 1, 2013, continue to have 15 years to use their benefits.
- In 2020, in response to concerns about the quality of certain for-profit education programs that target service members, Congress increased oversight and strengthened approval requirements. Congress also restored entitlements to service members who were affected by school closures and those who had enrolled in programs that were later found to have not met the standards to accept PGIB funds (Pub. L. 116-315, 2021).

---

[5] These requirements are mandated by Pub. L. 113-146, Section 702, 2014; Pub. L. 115-251, Section 301, 2018; and Pub. L. 117-68, 2021.

Target Population and Program Goals

PGIB beneficiaries are service members who served since September 11, 2001, and, in some cases, their family members. The legislation, which is similar to previous GI Bills, was intended to provide economic benefits to veterans, the military, and the nation. By this ratio- nale, in addition to helping veterans readjust to civilian life and facilitating military recruit- ment, both reducing veterans' reliance on other assistance by improving their postservice economic opportunities and investing in the education sector "reduce the costs of war" and "boost the economy" (Pub. L. 110-252, Title V, 2008).

The Congressional Research Service expounded on the enhancements in this new GI Bill, noting that the

> benefits were designed to meet four main objectives:
>
> - Provide reservists with benefits equivalent to those provided to members of the reg- ular Armed Forces for equivalent, though often not continuous, active duty service;
> - Ensure comprehensive educational benefits;
> - Meet military recruiting goals; and
> - Improve military retention through transferability of benefits (Dortch, 2021a, p. 1).

Citing a congressional hearing on the topics, the report added,

> Many Members of Congress hoped that a benefit that exceeded amounts available under the other active GI Bills would ameliorate the military recruiting challenges and higher unemployment rate among veterans compared with non-veterans of the same age group that existed in 2008 (Dortch, 2021a, p. 1).

Program Evaluation

In FY 2022, 564,501 beneficiaries received PGIB benefits, a 29-percent decrease from a high of 790,507 in FY 2015. Total expenditures were $8.1 billion in FY 2022, a 30-percent decline from a high of $11.6 billion in FY 2016 (Dortch, 2021a; VBA, 2023a). The reductions in PGIB participation and federal expenditures on PGIB benefits are the result of multiple factors, including the military drawdowns that occurred between 2010 and 2014 and led to significant force reductions (World Bank, 2020). The influx of transitioning service members and new veterans temporarily increased demand for PGIB benefits.

Figures 2.1 and 2.2 track federal spending on PGIB benefits and program participation, respectively, from the program's inception through FY 2022. The two figures roughly mirror each other and capture the program's buildup through 2016, and the subsequent drop-off in beneficiaries and overall spending reflects an overall declining veteran population. It is nota- ble that expenditures per beneficiary have remained relatively steady, despite the increasing cost of education, at between approximately $13,000 and $15,000 per year.

Although the federal government spends billions on PGIB benefits and there are hun- dreds of thousands of participants, little is known about the program's effects on military

FIGURE 2.1

PGIB Expenditures, by FY, 2010–2022

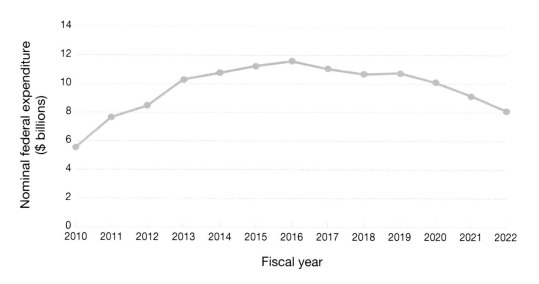

SOURCES: Features data from Dortch, 2021a, p. 26, Table 3; and VBA, 2023a, p. 157.

NOTE: The figure does not show expenditures for FY 2009 because the program launched in August 2009, or two months before the end of that FY.

FIGURE 2.2

PGIB Beneficiaries, by FY, 2010–2022

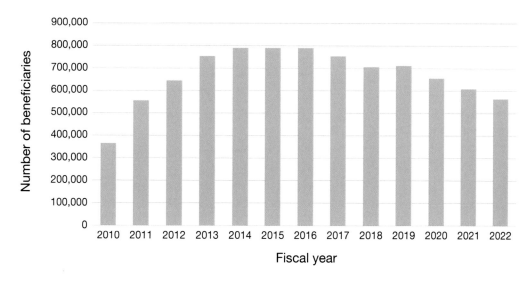

SOURCES: Features data from Dortch, 2021, p. 26, Table 3; and VBA, 2023a, p. 154.

NOTE: The figure does not show participation for FY 2009 because the program launched in August 2009, or two months before the end of that FY. Beneficiaries include service members, veterans, and dependents.

recruitment, retention, military-to-civilian transitions, or civilian-employment outcomes for veterans. Evaluations of the PGIB have focused primarily on the quality of the for-profit schools that have accounted for a large share of tuition reimbursements. In 2022, 27 percent of PGIB tuition funds went to for-profit schools (VBA, 2023a). After analyzing data from VA, a 2019 Congressional Budget Office report came to two significant conclusions.

- "For-profit schools have received a disproportionate share of money for tuition and fees relative to the number of Post-9/11 GI Bill students."
- In the seven years between the PGIB's inception and the report's release, "[h]ousing accounted for about half of annual total [VBA] spending. Tuition and fees were most of the rest" (Congressional Budget Office, 2019, p. ii).

Veteran Readiness and Employment (VR&E)

History and Policy

VR&E (formerly known as Vocational Rehabilitation and Employment) assists wounded veterans' return to civilian life. Pensions for disabled veterans date back to the colonial era, but efforts to help these veterans obtain gainful employment began after the Civil War, when the National Home for Disabled Volunteer Soldiers was established to provide vocational training, employment, and long-term residential care to Union veterans with service-connected injuries (National Park Service, 2017). World War I's advances in warfighting technology and medicine meant that a larger share of personnel survived their war injuries and returned home. The need to support these large numbers of disabled veterans motivated Congress to pass the landmark Vocational Rehabilitation Act—commonly known as the Smith-Sears Act—in 1918. The Smith-Sears Act provided disabled veterans with vocational guidance, job-placement and -adjustment services, training, and a subsistence allowance, as well as assistive devices that would allow them to work, such as prostheses (Pub. L. 65-178, 1918). In 1943, Congress established the framework for the modern VR&E when it provided disabled World War II veterans with up to four years of employment training and a subsistence allowance for program participants (Pub. L. 78-16, 1943).

In 1990, VR&E benefits were limited to veterans with a disability rating of 20 percent or more (Pub. L. 101-508, Section 8021, 1990, codified in U.S. Code, Title 38, Chapter 31, Section 3100, et seq.). In 1996, they were extended to those with a 10-percent disability rating and a serious employment handicap (Pub. L. 104-275, Section 101, 1996). In 2011, service members enrolled in a VR&E education program who were also eligible for the PGIB were allowed to elect to receive the PGIB housing allowance in lieu of the VR&E subsistence benefit (Pub. L. 111-377, 2011). In June 2020, the Vocational Rehabilitation and Employment program was relabeled as "Veterans Readiness and Employment" to better reflect the program's mission to help veterans achieve employment goals beyond vocational training and to reduce the stigma associated with the term *rehabilitation* (VA, 2020).[6]

Target Population and Program Goals

VR&E provides job training and other employment-related services to veterans with service-connected disabilities who face barriers to employment that impair a veteran's "ability to prepare for, pursue, or retain employment" (VBA, 2023a, p. 214). According to VBA, nearly 70 percent of VR&E participants have what it defines as "a serious employment handicap" (VBA, 2023a, p. 214), and these participants are eligible for adaptive accommodations and other additional services. Some of the services that VR&E provides, such as job search assistance and education benefits, are offered by other programs, including the TAP, MGIB, and PGIB.

To qualify for VR&E, a veteran must have a disability rating of 20 percent or more plus a barrier to employment or a disability rating of 10 percent plus a serious barrier to employment. Veterans work with vocational rehabilitation counselors to identify employment goals and chart a path to achieve them. The program provides both short-term assistance, such as helping veterans develop job search skills, and long-term assistance, including helping veterans acquire vocational skills, pursue education, or start a business (U.S. Code, Title 38, Chapter 31, Section 3100, et seq.).

When employment is not a viable option, VR&E provides independent living services. These services can include assistive technology, independent skills training, and connections to community-based services. Independent living services are provided for up to 24 months and can be extended in certain circumstances. By statute, no more than 2,700 veterans may be newly enrolled in independent living services each FY but this cap is rarely met (U.S. Code, Title 38, Chapter 31, Section 3120). In FY 2022, 234 veterans were enrolled in independent living (VBA, 2023a).

VR&E benefits can include a subsistence allowance during training or education or while the veteran is receiving independent living services. The amount of the subsistence allowance depends on whether the veteran is enrolled in services full time and the number of dependents. As of FY 2024, the rate could range from $193 to more than $1,300 per month (VBA, 2023b). A veteran receiving VR&E educational benefits might receive tuition reimbursement (which is paid directly to the school), as well as a subsistence allowance. A service member who is eligible for both VR&E and PGIB benefits can elect to receive the PGIB monthly housing allowance, which varies by location, in lieu of the VR&E subsistence allowance. When

---

[6] Throughout these discussions of benefits for disabled veterans, we refer to the term *disability ratings*, which are expressed as a percentage. For veterans, VA calculates these ratings based on the severity of a condition or injury or the degree of disability from multiple conditions or injuries—assigning a combined rating of up to 100-percent disabled. Veterans' eligibility for certain benefits depends on both their disability rating and their priority group, which is determined by several factors, including whether they have a service-connected disability. For more on VA disability ratings and how they are calculated, see VA (2022).

education benefits are provided under VR&E, counselors are allowed to approve a veteran's participation in a wide variety of programs, but veterans are required to select courses that are approved under the PGIB to the extent practicable. Unlike MGIB and PGIB education benefits, which last for 36 months, VR&E education benefits last up to 48 months and can be extended when deemed necessary to accomplish employment goals (Collins, 2021). VR&E participants can also receive interest-free loans to begin or continue the rehabilitation program. Eligible veterans have 12 years from the time of separation from the military or from the time they received a disability rating because of a service-connected disability to use their VR&E benefits.

Program Evaluation

In FY 2022, 105,054 veterans applied for VR&E services and 30,592 enrolled. A total of 124,437 veterans participated in the program in FY 2022, of whom 89,371 received a subsistence allowance. By the end of FY 2022, 11,810 had completed the program, and 8,514 had discontinued (VBA, 2023a, p. 212). Of that 11,810, more than 90 percent found employment, around 8 percent completed an education program, and 2 percent completed the independent living track (VBA, 2023a, p. 218). According to VBA, 85 percent of the veterans who moved on to a civilian job took on a professional, technical, or managerial role in FY 2022, the most recent year for which data were available. As shown in Table 2.1, the veterans who were hired

TABLE 2.1

Career Categories of VR&E Participants Who Entered the Civilian Workforce

Category	Number of Veterans	Average Annual Wages at Rehabilitation
Professional, technical, and managerial	9,335	$61,300
Machine trades	356	$44,611
Services	337	$47,463
Miscellaneous	344	$49,565
Clerical	231	$42,237
Structural (building trades)	244	$55,440
Sales	101	$40,838
Agricultural, fishery, and forest	42	$48,666
Processing (e.g., butcher, meat processor)	19	$34,244
Total number and average wage	11,009	$59,148

SOURCE: Features data from VBA, 2023a, p. 219.
NOTE: The table shows participants who completed the program and subsequently earned full-time wages. It does not include those who completed the independent living track, those who secured part-time employment, or those who pursued continuing education or volunteer work.

in this category of roles outearned their fellow program participants by $16,000 on average (VBA, 2023a, p. 219).

Total VR&E expenditures in FY 2022 were $1.47 billion. Nearly all of this funding was used for educational costs; 59 percent was used to cover costs for tuition, books, supplies, and fees, while 40 percent went to subsistence allowances (VBA, 2023a, pp. 7, 214). In 2004, VA formed a task force to evaluate VR&E which found little evidence that the program was effective in preparing veterans for employment (Fanning, 2008). Because of the lack of data on VR&E's long-term outcomes, in 2008, Congress required VA to conduct a 20-year longitudinal study of veterans who participated in the program (Pub. L. 110-389, Section 334, 2008). Overall, this study found that VR&E raised employment rates and earnings; additionally, veterans who completed the program had better health outcomes and were more likely to have health insurance.

DoD's Tuition Assistance Program

History and Policy

Starting with the Veterans Readjustment Benefits Act of 1966 (Pub. L. 89-358, 1966), VA education benefits have been extended to service members while they are still serving in the military. However, for a long time, DoD has had a separate program to reimburse service members' tuition for courses that they voluntarily pursue while off duty. DoD education benefits for active-duty service members began in the early 20th century, and their primary purpose was to develop an educated force capable of operating technically sophisticated military equipment.

By World War II, literacy had increased enough in the overall U.S. population that the Army imposed a literacy requirement on draftees. However, by 1943, facing a shortage of troops, the Army dropped this requirement and embarked on a robust and largely successful effort to teach literacy skills to recruits (Brandt, 2004). The Army established the Armed Forces Institute to connect soldiers with correspondence courses and to send them to civilian educational institutions. According to one researcher, the program's goals were not limited to developing force capabilities but also included "improv[ing] morale, and prepar[ing] personnel for eventual transition back to civilian life" (McGowan, 2012, p. 4).

After World War II, Army policy permitted soldiers to seek civilian education and reimbursed 75 percent of their tuition costs, up to a cap (Easterling, 1979). The 75-percent maximum reimbursement rate was later mandated by statute for all the military services (Pub. L. 92-570, Section 722, 1972). There have been various adjustments over time to what became known as DoD's Tuition Assistance Program, such as limiting benefits to enlisted or junior officers, imposing service commitments, and changing the reimbursement rate and cap. In 1984, the tuition reimbursement rate was raised to 90 percent for certain senior enlisted members, and, in 2000, Congress permitted—but did not require—the services to reimburse 100 percent of tuition with a minimum two-year service commitment for active-duty officers who received tuition assistance (Pub. L. 106-398, Section 1602, 2000). Currently, there are no service commitments for enlisted personnel, but the military services can require a commitment from enlisted reservists to serve up to an additional four years. For officers in the reserve component, the service obligation is four years (Kamarck, 2023).

Tuition assistance today is implemented through DoD Instruction (DoDI) 1322.25 (2020), *Voluntary Education Programs*, and DoDI 1322.19 (2020), *Voluntary Education Programs in Overseas Areas*, for overseas troops. These DoDIs require that tuition assistance be administered uniformly across the services but permit the services to establish their own eligibility criteria. DoD's Tuition Assistance Program permits voluntary off-duty education through institutions that are certified to participate in federal student aid. The program is voluntary, and service members typically require command approval before they can be reimbursed for courses. The services typically reimburse 100 percent of tuition up to certain caps, and students are required to maintain a GPA of 2.0 or higher. Tuition Assistance Program and PGIB benefits cannot be used to pay for the same course (DoDI 1322.19, 2020; DoDI 1322.25, 2020).

Target Population and Program Goals

DoD's Tuition Assistance Program is extended to active-duty and Selected Reserve service members of all ranks. The program helps service members complete high school, technical, and undergraduate- and graduate-level postsecondary education.

Tuition assistance as a recruitment tool intensified after 1973 when the U.S. military became an all-volunteer force.[7] The current incarnation of the program is intended to support multiple goals, including in-service force development, recruitment, readiness, and personal and professional advancement, although it is important to note that service members are not required to enroll in courses related to their military occupations (Kamarck, 2023). In a 2019 response to a request for data from Congress, GAO characterized DoD's position that "educational pursuits conducted off-duty prepare individuals to think critically, develop leadership skills, and acquire tools essential to meet 21st century challenges" (GAO, 2019b, p. 7).

Program Evaluation

Similar to evaluations of the PGIB and MGIB, evaluations of DoD's Tuition Assistance Program have focused on the quality of the participating schools, finding that DoD, similar to VA, could improve its oversight. In 2011, GAO found that DoD's process to review courses and services provided by schools was too narrow. For instance, DoD did not assess distance education, which accounted for 71 percent of the courses taken by service members in 2009. GAO faulted DoD for not overseeing school quality by tracking complaints or

---

[7] See, for example, Air Force Instruction 36-2306 (2021), which states that the purposes of tuition assistance are to support force development by maintaining an educated force and to support Air Force recruiting and retention efforts.

concerns from accrediting organizations (GAO, 2011). It made a similar finding three years later (GAO, 2014c). In 2019, it found that officers' periods of service after receiving tuition assistance benefits had increased but did not study the program's effect on officer retention (GAO, 2019b). There is also little evidence that DoD's Tuition Assistance Program has had an effect on military recruitment (Kamarck, 2023, p. 9). Program evaluations have generally not examined its effects on such key outcomes as force development, recruitment, retention, or connections between professional development during military service and postseparation transition outcomes.

Survivors' and Dependents' Educational Assistance (DEA)

History and Policy

The War Orphans' Educational Assistance Act of 1956 provided education benefits for 36 months to the children, up to age 23, of deceased service members who died in the line of duty or as a result of an injury or disease incurred during military service (Pub. L. 84-634, 1956). The law established what became the Dependents' Educational Assistance program, which later became known as the Survivors' and Dependents' Educational Assistance program.

In 2006, DEA was expanded to grant eligibility to the spouses and children of service members who were hospitalized or were receiving outpatient care for a permanent and total disability while still on active duty (Pub. L. 109-444, Section 3, 2006). In 2021, Congress required that approved postsecondary education programs may not charge DEA beneficiaries in excess of the in-state tuition and fees rate (Pub. L. 117-68, Section 2, 2021). The following year, Congress dropped the age and time limits for DEA benefits for those who qualified on or after August 1, 2023. Prior to that change, eligible children could use benefits up to age 26, and spouses had ten years to use them from the time that the service member was issued a 100-percent disability rating or 20 years after the service member's death (Pub. L. 117-328, Section 234, 2022). Prior to August 1, 2018, once beneficiaries began a course of study, they had 45 months to use the benefits. As of early 2024, benefits last for 36 months (U.S. Code, Title 38, Chapter 35, Section 3512).

Target Population and Program Goals

DEA provides education and training opportunities to eligible dependents (both spouses and children) of veterans who became totally disabled, died as a result of active-duty service, or were captured or went missing in the line of duty. The program's goals are to provide dependents with the education that they would have received if the service member were still able to earn wages (Dortch, 2017). The program covers tuition for approved programs of postsecondary education, career-training certificates, apprenticeships, and on-the-job training for up to 36 months. Similar to the MGIB, the program does not directly reimburse the cost of tuition; rather, the beneficiary receives a payment that is based on the type of education program being pursued and the number of courses being taken. In FY 2024, the maximum payment rate for full-time enrollment for postsecondary education was $1,488 per month (VA, 2023e).

Program Evaluation

GAO has studied the budgetary impact of DEA, along with other VA education programs. In FY 2022, 183,944 dependents received DEA benefits, up substantially from 109,760 in FY 2018, at a cost of $1.3 billion (VBA, 2018, p. 9; VBA, 2023a, p. 156). A 2018 GAO report noted that VA did not adequately oversee the quality of schools approved for VA education benefits, including DEA benefits (GAO, 2018b). The same GAO report also recommended that VA improve its program management, including communication and processing times. Little is known about postsecondary outcomes of DEA or any other VA education program, which has been a long-time criticism of DEA by GAO (see GAO, 2013).

CHAPTER 3

The Second-Tier Programs: MGIB and JVSG

The two employment transition programs that fall into the second tier in terms of the amount of federal funding they receive are (1) the MGIB, which is the predecessor to the PGIB and backed by dual policies for active-duty and Selected Reserve beneficiaries, and (2) JVSG, a federal grantmaking program that funds employment services at the state level. The MGIB differs from the PGIB in several ways and is being phased out. Among the most notable differences between the MGIB and PGIB from a budget standpoint are that service members contribute to their education funds and that MGIB benefits are not transferrable to dependents. MGIB benefits are also less generous overall than those under the PGIB, but they provide more flexibility by reimbursing service members and veterans directly.

The DOL-funded JVSG focuses specifically on connecting veterans and eligible spouses with career services and employment opportunities. Funding is allocated to the states, and beneficiaries receive priority services through specialists at American Job Center sites across the country. This means that beneficiaries can access the expansive resources of DOL with the support of dedicated staff who have been trained on the unique challenges and needs of this population.

The Montgomery GI Bill (MGIB)

History and Policy

There are two MGIBs, one for those meeting qualifying active-duty service and another for qualifying Selected Reserve service. The larger of the two programs is the MGIB–Active Duty, which is codified in U.S. Code, Title 38, Chapter 30. The smaller program is the MGIB–Selected Reserve for those qualifying Selected Reserve service, which is codified in U.S. Code, Title 10, Chapter 1606. Both MGIBs provide eligible service members with funding to assist with tuition and other expenses associated with postsecondary education and training. MGIB–Active Duty provides a higher level of benefits, which must be used within ten years of separation. MGIB–Selected Reserve must be used while the reservist is still serving. To be eligible for the MGIB–Active Duty, service members must elect to contribute $1,200 ($100 per month) during their first year on active duty; the MGIB–Selected Reserve requires no such contribution beyond the service requirements discussed in the next section.

All beneficiaries receive up to 36 monthly payments for eligible education or training, and most MGIB–Active Duty participants are provided with "a monthly subsistence allowance, but additional payments are available for tutorial assistance, qualified test fees, Tuition Assistance Top-Up, supplemental assistance, and the Buy-Up program" (Dortch, 2021b, p. 12).[1] Standard benefit levels under MGIB–Active Duty for beneficiaries with at least three years on active duty in FY 2024 were $2,358 per month during full-time enrollment for subsistence, tuition and fees, supplies, books, and equipment (VA, 2023c). Standard benefit levels under MGIB–Selected Reserve in FY 2024 were $466 per month during full-time enrollment for subsistence, tuition and fees, supplies, books, and equipment (VA, 2023d).

Both the MGIBs were established by the Department of Defense Authorization Act of 1985 (Pub. L. 98-525, 1984). Congress has increased benefit amounts several times, and "[s]ince FY2004, MGIB-AD [Active Duty] benefits have been adjusted annually according to the CPI [Consumer Price Index]" (Smole and Loane, 2008, p. 12). Nonetheless, even as far back as 2007, the Congressional Research Service noted that benefits had not risen as quickly as tuition expenses (Mercer and Skinner, 2007, p. 11). The PGIB is gradually replacing the MGIB. Section 1004 of the Johnny Isakson and David P. Roe, M.D., Veterans Health Care and Benefits Improvement Act of 2020 (Pub. L. 116-315, 2020) phases out the MGIB: There will be no new enrollees after September 30, 2030, but those eligible for the program prior to that date will be able to use their benefits until ten years after they leave the service.

Target Population and Program Goals

Both MGIBs target service members who are currently serving on active duty or in the Selected Reserve, as well as recently separated veterans. Eligibility for MGIB–Selected Reserve is limited to "Selected Reservists, including National Guard members, who enlist, re-enlist, or extend an enlistment for six years after June 30, 1985, and reserve officers who agree to serve an additional six years above any existing obligation" (Dortch, 2021b, p. 10).

Eligibility for MGIB–Active Duty benefits is limited to those who join the military for the first time before October 1, 2030, and meet one of the requirements for years of active-duty service, depending on service-connected disability status and Selected Reserve commitment. Service members who served as officers and who either attended a service academy or received a Reserve Officer Training Corps scholarship are not eligible for either MGIB program, and benefits are not transferable to dependents under the MGIB.

---

[1] The Tuition Assistance Top-Up Program allows service members to use PGIB and MGIB benefits to cover tuition costs beyond what is covered under the Tuition Assistance Program. *Supplemental assistance* refers to an additional housing or subsistence allowance of up to $950 per month for active-duty service members and $350 per month for reservists who agree to a longer service commitment or pursue specific types of training (i.e., critical skills). The Buy-Up Program is a benefit under the MGIB–Active Duty in which the federal government matches up to $600 in monthly contributions beyond the $1,200 that service members elect to contribute to participate in the program. Each $1 contribution by the service member is matched by up to $9 in benefits (Dortch, 2021b, pp. 5–6, 25–26).

Both MGIBs were designed to support the military in its goals of "recruiting and retaining a highly qualified all-volunteer force—active duty, Reserves, and National Guard" (Dortch, 2011, p. 11). Some witnesses in congressional hearings have argued that the MGIB's predecessor, the Post-Vietnam Era Veterans Educational Assistance Program, required a contribution from service members that was too high to successfully boost retention. To address this criticism, the MGIB–Active Duty reduced the contribution requirement, and the MGIB–Selected Reserve requires no contribution, but service members must extend their service commitment to receive benefits.

Program Evaluation

The fact that service members must choose to contribute $1,200 to be eligible for the MGIB–Active Duty makes it particularly difficult to overcome selection bias when evaluating this program.[2] Simon, Negrusa, and Warner (2010) addressed this challenge by measuring the effects of changes in benefit amounts as a result of congressional action that occurred after service members had made their contribution decisions. The authors found that an increase in higher education benefits was associated with an increase in benefit use *and* increased rates of separation from active duty, specifically in the Army and Air Force (Simon, Negrusa, and Warner, 2010). The authors note that although these types of education benefits have been shown to attract high-quality recruits, these recruits are "more likely to separate after their initial enlistment [period] and more likely to use their educational benefits" within two years of separation (Simon, Negrusa, and Warner, 2010, p. 1009). The implication is that these benefits serve as an incentive to enlist but also as an incentive to separate from the military to pursue other education and training. To provide additional insights into who has used MGIB benefits, an observational regression analysis of data from the 2001 National Survey of Veterans did not find evidence that the MGIB increased the enrollment of disabled Gulf War veterans in higher education (Smith-Osborne, 2009).

Jobs for Veterans State Grant (JVSG)

History and Policy

JVSG funds veteran employment-support services at 54 workforce agencies in all U.S. states, Washington, D.C., and U.S. territories. The program entitles veterans and eligible surviving spouses to priority of service to DOL-funded employment and training programs. Grant funding provided under JVSG is proportional to a given state workforce agency's share of vet-

---

[2] This section specifically reviews evidence on the effects of the MGIB on veterans' outcomes. For a review of the effects of the MGIB on recruitment and retention, see Asch, Hosek, and Warner (2007).

erans seeking employment.[3] The program is authorized under U.S. Code, Title 38, Chapter 41, and is administered by DOL's Veterans' Employment and Training Service (DOL, undated-a).

The Workforce Innovation and Opportunity Act of 2014 established a nationwide network of approximately 2,300 American Job Centers that offer DOL-funded employment services to the general population, such as training referrals, career counseling, job listings, job matching, job fairs, and résumé-writing support (DOL, undated-b). JVSG funds dedicated staff at these centers—and funded the same positions at the American Job Centers' predecessor state-level offices prior to 2014—"to provide individualized career- and training-related services to veterans and eligible persons with significant barriers to employment (SBEs), as well as other authorized populations, and help employers fill their workforce needs with job-seeking veterans" (National Veterans' Training Institute, 2022, p. 7). The program specifically funds two types of dedicated staff positions:

- Disabled Veterans' Outreach Program personnel provide employment services to disabled and other high-need veterans. Such services include case management, career guidance, staff-assisted job searches, and labor market information.
- Local veterans' employment representatives "perform outreach to local employers, conduct employment workshops for veterans, and work with other AJC [American Job Center] personnel to provide employment-related services to veterans" (Collins, Bradley, and Isaacs, 2019, p. 8).

JVSG was created by the Jobs for Veterans Act in 2002 by legislatively linking several existing programs. Local veterans' employment representatives have existed since the Servicemen's Readjustment Act of 1944 (Pub. L. 78-346, 1944), and the Veterans' Rehabilitation and Education Amendments of 1980 (Pub. L. 96-466, 1980) codified the Disabled Veterans' Outreach Program in U.S. Code, Title 38, Chapter 41, Section 4103A. Representatives are federally managed positions under the Assistant Secretary of Labor for Veterans' Employment and Training (U.S. Code, Title 38, Chapter 41, Section 4102A).

Other forms of employment support were available through the Vietnam Era Veterans' Readjustment Assistance Act of 1972 (Pub. L. 92-540, 1972), which entitled veterans from the Vietnam War era and their qualifying spouses to priority employment services, and through the Jobs for Veterans Act (Pub. L. 107-288, 2002), which reoriented existing programs to allow local implementation with federal oversight and funding. Specifically, the Jobs for Veterans Act "revised Chapters 41–43 of Title 38 [of the U.S. Code] to give states more latitude in the conduct of their DVOP [Disabled Veterans' Outreach Program] staff and LVER [local

---

[3] The DOL (undated-a) describes the funding allocation for JVSG as follows:

Several states receive a minimum amount of funding to ensure that a certain level of staff can be maintained, particularly in states with remote pockets of Native Americans and a large number of sparsely populated rural counties.

veterans' employment representatives] and placed more emphasis on accountability" (Tennessee Department of Labor and Workforce Development, 2017, p. 3).

Target Population and Program Goals

JVSG prioritizes "disabled veterans and veterans who served on active duty during a war or in a campaign or expedition for which a campaign badge has been authorized" (U.S. Code, Title 38, Chapter 41, Section 4102). "Eligible persons" include spouses of veterans with a 100-percent disability rating resulting from a service-connected disability and the spouses of those who died of a service-connected disability, are missing in action, or were captured in line of duty (U.S. Code, Title 38, Chapter 41, Section 4101). Additional JVSG funding supports transitioning service members who have participated in the TAP and require individualized career services (National Veterans' Training Institute, 2022).

The Jobs for Veterans Act clearly outlined the goals of the program in modifying Title 38, Chapter 41, of the U.S. Code as follows:

> The Congress declares as its intent and purpose that there shall be an effective (1) job and job training intensive services program, (2) employment placement service program, and (3) job training placement service program for eligible veterans and eligible persons . . . so as to provide such veterans and persons the maximum of employment and training opportunities . . . [and] to ease the transition of service members to civilian careers that are consistent with, or an outgrowth of, the military experience of the servicemembers (U.S. Code, Title 38, Chapter 41, Section 4102).

Program Evaluation

Although there have been several analyses of the effects of JVSG, none have been randomized or pseudo-randomized evaluations. Most analyses have examined compliance with the Jobs for Veterans Act's priority-access provisions and have generally found that this legislative requirement has been implemented appropriately (Boraas, Roemer, and Bodenlos, 2013; Rosenberg et al., 2015). One direct analysis of JVSG outcomes was conducted by Thompson and colleagues in 2015. DOL collects and publishes performance data on each state's DOL-funded employment services programs, including quarterly data on active program participants and for three quarters after program participation (DOL, undated-d). Thompson and colleagues (2015) used these data to compare employment and wage outcomes for JVSG veterans, non-JVSG veterans, and nonveterans. They also compared outcomes by gender, age, and military separation status, as well as across states. They used regression analysis to control for some observable demographic features that could correlate with both program participation and employment outcomes, concluding that

> JVSG veterans exhibit higher rates of employment and higher earnings after exiting the program compared to non-JVSG veterans and non-veterans. JVSG veterans also exhibit smaller gender wage gaps. JVSG veterans generally receive staff-assisted services more

quickly than non-veterans do, which may be an indicator of success for priority of service (POS) legislation (Thompson et al., 2015, p. i).

Thompson and colleagues found that JVSG veterans had a 48-percent employment rate and mean earnings of $20,625 in the first nine months after completing the program, compared with a 47-percent employment rate and mean earnings of $19,654 for nonveterans.[4] They also found substantial differences across states in wage and employment outcomes for program participants.

The outcomes of Thompson et al. (2015) are noncausal and could reflect a combination of JVSG effects and unobserved differences among the comparison groups. However, their results mirror findings from an analysis published in 2010 by Trutko and Barnow, who found that veterans who participated in the DOL Adult and Dislocated Worker Program before the priority-of-service provisions went into effect had higher wages than nonveterans, both before and after program participation. The authors speculated that these outcomes "may reflect that veterans enrolling in WIA [the Adult and Dislocated Worker Program] come to the program with more work-related experience and educational qualifications—and hence, perhaps also may have less need (or desire) for training services" (Trutko and Barnow, 2010, p. 21). In short, even though veterans participating in DOL-funded employment services under JVSG appear to have relatively positive employment outcomes compared with nonveteran participants in other DOL-funded programs, it is unknown whether those outcomes are the result of JVSG itself or preexisting differences between veteran and nonveteran program participants.

---

[4] Note that the authors did not report variance for any study outcomes, so it was not possible to evaluate the statistical significance of these findings.

CHAPTER 4

The Third-Tier Program: DoD TAP

The 1990s saw a significant drawdown of U.S. military forces as the country shifted its focus from the Cold War to a new era of global engagement. This drawdown was driven by a variety of factors, including changing geopolitical realities, budget constraints, and shifting public opinion about the role of the military in U.S. foreign policy.

When the Soviet Union collapsed in 1991, the United States no longer faced a direct military threat from a rival superpower. That year, the U.S. military had approximately 2.1 million active-duty and reserve personnel (World Bank, 2020). By 2001, the size of the U.S. military had decreased to approximately 1.4 million personnel (World Bank, 2020). According to GAO (1994, p. 1), in each year from 1990 to 1993, approximately 300,000 service members were separating from the military.

A significant number of personnel who would have preferred to continue serving were forced to leave during the drawdown. The drawdown increased the number of veterans pushed into the civilian labor market and created a significant increase in the supply of workers with military skills. Additionally, the early stages of the drawdown coincided with the 1991–1992 recession, when unemployment was relatively high and job openings were generally scarce. One consequence was a high unemployment rate for veterans, and many veterans had limited success in finding work that matched their skill sets. The TAP was established in anticipation of the drawdown's effects on service members and their families.

History and Policy

In 1990, Congress established a program to assist transitioning service members affected by the military drawdown as part of the National Defense Authorization Act for Fiscal Year 1991 (Pub. L. 101-510). Early evidence indicated that the TAP was poorly designed and implemented because the program had virtually no infrastructure to identify who would likely be transitioning, which services would be helpful, or how to deliver those services. An early GAO evaluation of the TAP found that that DoD, the military services, and commanders were not adequately supporting the program and preventing beneficiaries from accessing "timely transition services as required by law," and the GAO report furthermore claimed that

[a]s a result of this lack of support

- officials responsible for providing transition services did not know who was separating,
- separating service members were not being provided information translating their military experience and training into marketable civilian skills,
- members were either not being provided individual preseparation counseling or were not receiving it timely, and
- many service members and their spouses did not have the opportunity to attend transition seminars and use employment assistance centers (GAO, 1994, pp. 1–2).

GAO found that DoD did not follow the law by failing to provide separating service members with skills verification documents that would aid in translating their military skills and training into civilian jobs (Pub. L. 101-510, 1990). Form DD 2586, *Verification of Military Education and Training*, is now used to collect this information. According to GAO, nearly 500,000 service members had transitioned before DoD produced a skills verification document (GAO, 1994, p. 5). Even as late as 1994, many service members were not receiving such documentation—four years after the law went into effect. By 1996, there was sufficient evidence that the transition process was not running effectively and that Congress needed to establish a commission to identify opportunities to improve it.

The 1996 Congressional Commission on Servicemembers and Veterans Transition Assistance found that the existing transition-assistance programs were inadequate. The commission's report served as a critical assessment of these programs' shortcomings and emphasized the need for significant changes to better support military personnel and veterans as they transitioned to civilian life. Overall, the report was highly critical of DoD, DOL, and VA for their lack of coordination and communication. The commissioners wrote,

> It is absolutely unacceptable that the unemployment rate for newly separated veterans, men and women who are dedicated, mature, skilled, trained, disciplined, experienced, trustworthy and drug free, exceeds that of non-veterans the same age by over 20 percent.

> The programs and institutions entrusted with the responsibility for veterans' employment have failed (Congressional Commission on Servicemembers and Veterans Transition Assistance, 1999, p. 5).

The report also criticized existing programs for not providing personalized assistance to military personnel and veterans, which caused many to struggle to adjust to civilian life.

The commission's report recommended that DoD and VA collaborate to develop a comprehensive transition-assistance program that included job training, education, and counseling services. The report also recommended that DoD and VA improve their coordination and communication, provide more-personalized assistance, and increase their outreach efforts to ensure that military personnel and veterans were aware of the available resources and services.

The VOW to Hire Heroes Act of 2011 (Pub. L. 112-56, Title II, 2011) made several key changes to the TAP to better support transitioning service members and veterans, such as the following:

- **Mandatory participation:** The TAP became mandatory for all service members who are separating from the military.
- **Expanded services:** The services offered through the TAP now include job-search assistance, education and training opportunities, and counseling on VA benefits and services.
- **Personalized assistance:** The TAP was redesigned to provide more-personalized assistance to service members and veterans, including individualized counseling and support services.
- **Preseparation counseling:** Separating service members receive preseparation counseling at least 365 days before their separation date to help them prepare for the transition to civilian life.
- **Follow-up services:** The TAP now provides follow-up services to service members and veterans after they have completed the program if they fail to meet career readiness standards.

Overall, the VOW to Hire Heroes Act of 2011 made significant changes to better support transitioning service members and veterans and to ensure that they have the resources and support they need to successfully transition to civilian life. These results are discussed in a GAO report that examined the cost-benefit calculus of the TAP redesign (GAO, 2016). Figure 4.1 offers a helpful illustration of the TAP's process and typical timeline for Department of the Air Force personnel and their dependents.

Target Population

Mandatory TAP participation became policy in 2011 with passage of the VOW to Hire Heroes Act of 2011 (Pub. L. 112-56, Title II, 2011). Service members who serve at least 180 continuous days on active duty must participate in certain components of the TAP. This mandate for active-duty participation has been problematic for the reserve component: If guardsmen or reservists were activated for 180 days or more, they would be required to attend the TAP. Demobilization happens quickly and without much notice, making it nearly impossible for these service members to attend TAP courses before leaving the military. Lengthening of the coursework by two days only exacerbated the problem. This issue was broadly discussed in a 2005 GAO report with the subtitle, *Enhanced Services Could Improve Transition Assistance for Reserves and National Guard*. The requirements posed an additional challenge for small and remote bases that had only a few hundred separations each year. It is difficult to staff and host courses at facilities where only a few service members separate each week (GAO, 2021).

FIGURE 4.1

TAP Roadmap for Transitioning Airmen and Eligible Dependents

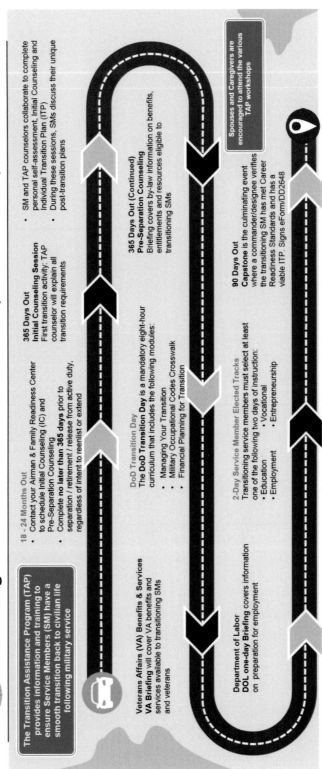

Transition Assistance Program Program Roadmap

Program Directives: Title 10 U.S.C., DoDI 1332.35, DAFI 36-3009

The Transition Assistance Program (TAP) provides information and training to ensure Service Members (SM) have a smooth transition back to civilian life following military service

18 - 24 Months Out
- Contact your Airman & Family Readiness Center to schedule Initial Counseling (IC) and Pre-Separation Counseling
- Complete no later than 365 days prior to separation / retirement / release from active duty, regardless of intent to reenlist or extend

365 Days Out
Initial Counseling Session
First transition activity; TAP counselor will explain all transition requirements

- SM and TAP counselors collaborate to complete personal self-assessment, Initial Counseling and Individual Transition Plan (ITP)
- During these sessions, SMs discuss their unique post-transition plans

365 Days Out (Continued)
Pre-Separation Counseling
Briefing covers by-law information on benefits, entitlements and resources eligible to transitioning SMs

DoD Transition Day
The **DoD Transition Day** is a mandatory eight-hour curriculum that includes the following modules:
- Managing Your Transition
- Military Occupational Codes Crosswalk
- Financial Planning for Transition

90 Days Out
Capstone is the culminating event where a commander/designee verifies the transitioning SM has met Career Readiness Standards and has a viable ITP. Signs eForm/DD2648

Veterans Affairs (VA) Benefits & Services
VA Briefing will cover VA benefits and services available to transitioning SMs and veterans

2-Day Service Member Elected Tracks
Transitioning service members must select at least one of the following two days of instruction:
- Education
- Vocational
- Employment
- Entrepreneurship

Spouses and Caregivers are encouraged to attend the various TAP workshops

Department of Labor
DOL one-day Briefing covers information on preparation for employment

Integrity - Service - Excellence

SOURCE: Reproduced from Scott Air Force Base Military and Family Readiness Center, undated.

NOTE: DAF = Department of the Air Force.

One other significant change has been the role of the TAP for spouses. Each service branch has a family-support program that offers employment services similar to the TAP. Additionally, all TAP materials are available online, and spouses can elect to attend classes.

Program Goals

In the 33 years since the TAP was established by Congress, the program's goals have changed considerably. In its earliest iterations, the TAP's primary goal was to help newly separated veterans find suitable employment. The basic sessions provided information about civilian jobs, how to write a résumé, and how to translate military skills to civilian jobs. Although all service members were thought to benefit from such a program, policymakers viewed those who were being involuntarily separated from the military as a result of the drawdown as most at risk of joblessness. The TAP was also understood to benefit DoD directly by maintaining the viability of the all-volunteer force (Congressional Commission on Servicemembers and Veterans Transition Assistance, 1999).

Self-Assessment and Counselor's Evaluation

The current iteration of the TAP is quite different than how it started. First and foremost, the program requires the service member to complete a self-assessment and record post-transition goals. Counselors then gauge service members' preparedness to transition and assign them to one of three tiers: Tier 1 is fully prepared for transition, tier 2 is moderately prepared, and tier 3 is not prepared. After identifying which track the separating service member will take, the focus is on targeting resources to those who are least prepared to transition (i.e., tiers 2 and 3). After the self-assessment and counselor's evaluation, the service member is given a briefing about the TAP process and benefits, services, and resources that will be available to them during their transition.

Core Curriculum and Two-Day Instruction

The core curriculum consists of three days of typically in-person classes. One day is dedicated to DoD transition services and includes information about the crosswalk of military to civilian occupations, financial literacy, and resiliency. A second day is spent on VA benefits and services and includes a briefing on how to check benefit eligibility, how to apply for benefits, and how to use benefits. The third and final day of the core curriculum is spent with DOL representatives on civilian employment fundamentals, including a broad overview of employment in the civilian labor market.

Tier 2 and tier 3 service members (depending on their service branch) are required to take an additional two-day class focused on one of four career tracks: employment, education, vocational, or entrepreneurship.[1] Service members classified as tier 1 (i.e., fully prepared for transition) are not required to take this two-day sequence of classes, although they can elect to do so.

The TAP now recognizes that service members have different pathways out of the military (e.g., schooling, apprenticeships, employment, starting a business, retirement), and that the program's goal is broader than helping service members transition to civilian jobs. In some ways, this makes the current iteration of the TAP significantly better than its predecessors, but it can also make service delivery more complicated—especially at small installations where few people are transitioning into relatively rare tracks, such as entrepreneurship.

Program Evaluation

Since the final report from the Congressional Commission on Servicemembers and Veterans Transition Assistance was released in 1999, GAO has written about veteran employment and the TAP in 2002, 2005, 2011, 2012, 2014, and in every year from 2018 to 2023. Many its reports have been critical of the TAP. A selection of these reports' subtitles gives a sense of the program's deficiencies: *Better Targeting, Coordinating, and Reporting Needed to Enhance Program Effectiveness* (GAO, 2012), *Improved Oversight Needed to Enhance Implementation of Transition Assistance Program* (GAO, 2014b), *Coast Guard Needs to Improve Data Quality and Monitoring of Its Transition Assistance Program* (GAO, 2018a), and—even more directly—*DOD Needs to Improve Performance Reporting and Monitoring for the Transition Assistance Program* (GAO, 2017). By 2022, DoD had taken many steps toward helping service members transfer their skills to the civilian labor market, and, by 2023, its information systems were deemed reliable enough to track program participation, according to congressional testimony by a GAO official (Locke, 2023; GAO, 2022; GAO, 2023).

One comprehensive evaluation of the TAP was conducted by researchers from ICF Incorporated, LLC, for DOL's Chief Evaluation Office (O'Conner, Schoeneberger, and Clark, 2023). The study compared transitioned Army personnel who attended the three-day DOL employment workshop between 2014 and 2019 with those who did not. Overall, the researchers found that workshop attendance was associated with several outcomes: Workshop participants found jobs more quickly, remained employed longer, and had lower unemployment rates one year after separation from the military—although not at six months after separation—but they also earned *less* in wages. However, starting the TAP earlier in the transition process and attending sessions on VA benefits and financial planning were associated with higher wages for the workshop participants, particularly the 40 percent who completed the workshop six months or more before separation (O'Conner, Schoeneberger, and Clark, 2023, p. 69).

---

[1] All tier 3 service members are required to select a career track and attend the associated two-day class. The service branches have adopted different policies related to tier 2 service members. The Navy and Air Force do not their require attendance, while the Army and Marine Corps make these decisions on an individual basis.

The lower civilian wages of veterans who completed the TAP workshop could reflect a sense of urgency that was instilled by their participation and led them to accept a job before they understood the value of their skills in the job market. However, standard economic theory suggests that after they gathered new information, they would leave that position in favor of one with higher pay. Yet, the report suggests that these workers remained employed in the same role for a longer period than their nonparticipant peers, and that their wages were consistently lower on average at each wave of data collection. The authors of the evaluation posit that participants' greater likelihood to pursue higher education after separation and difficulty finding civilian work that aligned with their military skills has a dampening effect on earning potential in the years after transitioning (O'Conner, Schoeneberger, and Clark, 2023, p. 80). According to what we know from research on youth job training programs, such as the Job Corps, a first-quarter postseparation difference of $3,000 between TAP course participants and those who opted out is likely not attributable to the effects of a three-day course on civilian employment. Job Corps programs last many months, and participants typically have small increases in earnings relative to the control groups (Schochet, Burghardt, and McConnell, 2008).

Prior studies of the TAP suggest that the program has had some long-term effects. The TAP has been associated with higher labor force participation and higher educational attainment, which possibly reflects an increased awareness of PGIB and MGIB benefits but has no statistically significant relationship with higher wages (Li, 2018). Silva (2011) highlights some demographic differences in TAP participation but finds no overall evidence that participation has a positive effect on employment outcomes. Other studies, such as Sadacca et al. (1995), show mixed results: Attending a TAP course offered by DOL is associated with lower wages, but participation in non-DOL courses is associated with higher wages. Transitioning service members are not randomly assigned to the TAP, and none of these studies could account for unobservable factors that influenced TAP participation, such as individual motivation, or differences in baseline preparedness for the labor market between TAP participants and nonparticipants. Self-selection into treatment will generally cause bias in the estimated effects of a program, and this bias limits the evidence for the TAP's performance.

Since the TAP's inception, the guidance has been for separating service members to begin planning for their transition early. Past guidance was to begin 90 days before separation, and then that recommendation was lengthened to 180 days. Current guidance is to begin preparing one to two *years* prior to separation and attend the capstone briefing no less than 90 days before the separation date. There are certainly reasons to prepare service members for the civilian labor market earlier in their military careers. SkillBridge is a DoD program that allows active-duty service members to spend their last six months on duty in an apprenticeship at a civilian business or other organization. However, there is simply no rigorous quantitative evidence that starting the transition process earlier in a military career will lead to better civilian labor market outcomes.

In 2020, DoD consolidated office functions to establish the Military-Civilian Transition Office to oversee TAP implementation. Other new TAP design features make a good quasi-experimental research design possible. For example, the Navy and the Air Force have different policies from the Army and the Marine Corps for whether a separating tier-2 service member has to attend a two-day career path class. Future studies could examine the algorithm that assigns tiers and compare service members who are just above the threshold for career readiness with those who are below it. However, we acknowledge that this approach would test only the treatment effect of the two-day class, because all separating service members are required to attend the basic TAP courses.

Finally, DoD is in the process of merging its data with the U.S. Census Bureau. As a result, researchers will be able to more easily link military experience with civilian labor market outcomes, including the timing of when the TAP is completed and whether any of the two-day courses are taken.

As we have noted previously, during the years since GAO conducted its audit of 45 programs, little has changed in the employment transition-assistance landscape. With the exception of a few pilot programs, there had been no new additions. However, there is a program that appears poised for a wider-scale launch, which is profiled in the box below. The Employment Navigator and Partnership Program (ENPP), which DOL is piloting to address some of the civilian employment challenges that transitioning service members and spouses face, is available to transitioning service members and spouses at selected bases who have participated in the TAP.

ENPP: Individualized Career Counseling and Guidance

The ENPP connects transitioning service members and spouses with employment navigators who can provide job-matching services, assist with referrals to veteran-friendly employers and apprenticeships, find hiring and networking events, and match jobseekers with training opportunities, placement services, mentors, and community-based wrap-around services. To be eligible, service members and spouses must participate in the TAP at one of the locations where the pilot program is offered, but DOL operates the program outside the TAP process. The ENPP is available up to two years before separation and up to one year postseparation (DOL, undated-c). At the time of this writing, the program had partnered with 52 service providers, including veteran-serving organizations, large-scale job boards (e.g., Indeed), and corporate training and placement programs.

In 2021, DOL's Chief Evaluation Office commissioned an evaluation of the ENPP that appeared to involve data collection through a series of focus groups, but the findings have not been released (White House, Office of Management and Budget, 2022). For this reason, we did not include the ENPP in our analysis, but it is worth mentioning here as a potential enhancement to the TAP that can provide longer-term, individualized employment support and help to overcome some of the potential shortfalls of the TAP.

CHAPTER 5

The Small Programs: History and Performance

The vast majority of federal transition assistance funding goes to the programs discussed in Chapters 2–4. However, no analysis of the employment transition-support landscape would be complete without a deeper dive into the dozens of other programs that collectively receive millions of dollars in federal funding to assist transitioning service members and veterans. There is overlap both among these programs and with the larger federal programs they supplement, but many small programs explicitly address gaps in support or enhance the outcomes of other programs. Some of the best ideas in transition assistance are happening at a smaller scale. This is especially true in apprenticeship and job-matching programs, in which VA, DoD, and even the U.S. Department of Agriculture (USDA) have been taking concrete, practical steps to connect transitioning veterans with career opportunities in the dynamic civilian labor market.

To provide a clearer picture of the diversity of smaller programs that receive federal funding to support military-to-civilian employment transitions, this chapter groups the programs by their primary goals as follows:

- **General education and employment counseling programs** help transitioning service members and veterans build life plans and assess their education and employment needs and preferences.
- **Education-focused programs** might overlap with the larger programs previously discussed in this report. But in this chapter, we look specifically at small programs that provide funding, counseling, and accreditation for military skills.
- **Employment-focused programs** had three overarching objectives: building employment skills, assisting with job searches and on-the-job employer interactions, and connecting transitioning service members and veterans with jobs or apprenticeships.
- **Transition programs for nonveterans**—typically the family members—help transitioning service members and veterans maintain a strong support network and recognize that readjusting to civilian life is a challenge for those who did not, themselves, serve. We also included in this category **general benefit support programs** that help veterans access benefits that are not directly related to education or employment.

The large number of programs meant that we chose to focus on the broad ideas behind each rather than the specifics of their implementation. A few of these programs are unique in that they provide federal grants to organizations that carry out their program objectives instead of engaging in these activities directly.

General Education and Employment Counseling Programs

The TAP, which we discuss in Chapter 4, has a significant counseling component, including specific days dedicated to transitioning service members' choice of education, employment, or entrepreneurship. Although VA, DOL, and the U.S. Department of Education (ED) provide ongoing transition-focused education and employment counseling, small programs dedicated to employment training and counseling are generally distributed between VA and the U.S. Small Business Administration (SBA). The following programs serve a broad cross section of transitioning service members and veterans:

- VA's **Personalized Career Planning and Guidance** program provides counseling to help veterans identify and plan to achieve education and career goals.
- DoD's **Military OneSource** also covers many of the basics of career planning by providing "comprehensive information, referral, and assistance," as well as assistance with taxes, financial planning, and other needs that are not always addressed by other programs (MyArmyBenefits, undated).
- DoD's **Yellow Ribbon Reintegration Program** provides information about benefits (especially military benefits) to transitioning service members and their families. This program also provides eligible nonveterans with access to TAP training.

Education-Focused Programs

Funding

Most education funding is provided by the larger programs discussed in previous chapters—most notably the MGIB, PGIB, and DoD's Tuition Assistance Program. Only a few small programs are directly involved with undergraduate education funding; some, such as the VA Work-Study Program (which we discuss in the section "Job Matching and On-the-Job Training") help veterans find work while they pursue an education. However, these large programs cannot not address the needs of all veterans, particularly those who would benefit from greater flexibility or additional funding, and the following programs focus on addressing these needs:

- VA's **Tuition Assistance Top-Up** benefit directly addresses this need for flexibility by allowing military students to use MGIB or PGIB benefits to cover the tuition costs in excess of those covered by DoD's Tuition Assistance Program. It does not provide direct funding beyond that already provided under the MGIB or PGIB; it simply empowers military students to use that money in ways that serve their education goals.

- VA's **Reserve Educational Assistance Program** similarly allowed reservists to use MGIB or PGIB funds for education. This program expired in 2015, and benefits for enrollees ceased in 2019. However, some veterans who were eligible for this program might be eligible for similar benefits under the PGIB.

Counseling

A variety of programs provide high-level life counseling that could include advice on education planning. We attempt to categorize such programs as granularly as possible, highlighting those that focus on career or vocational counseling, because our goal is to assess the landscape of *employment*-focused transition assistance. However, a few counseling programs are dedicated to education and can help veterans identify the coursework or degrees they need to complete to pursue specific civilian careers:

- VA's **VetSuccess on Campus** epitomizes this focus on education. Participating postsecondary institutions have a VA counselor who helps student veterans adjust to life on campus, including serving as an advocate for student veterans and assisting them in applying for VA benefits. These counselors can also arrange for disability accommodations and referrals to physical and mental health services.
- VA's **Veterans Integration to Academic Leadership** program directly provides mental health assistance and on-campus clinical services for veterans with such support as time-management assistance and traumatic brain-injury recovery (VA, 2023f). Similar to VetSuccess on Campus, this program helps veterans access other VA benefits and promotes campus policies and practices that better serve veterans' needs.
- Veterans are eligible for many of the same ED programs that serve the general population. However, we have identified two that target veterans specifically. **Centers of Excellence for Veteran Student Success** and **Veterans Upward Bound** are both administered as grants to accredited organizations. Centers of Excellence for Veteran Success operates similarly to the two VA programs in this section in that it provides on-campus assistance to promote veterans' academic success, including counseling, tutoring, and help with the application process. Meanwhile, the Veterans Upward Bound program is offered outside college campuses. Its free education services have a precollege focus, mostly directing veterans to prerequisite coursework and counseling on the college application process. Veterans Upward Bound is part of a broader swathe of ED programs that have historically helped disadvantaged populations navigate postsecondary education opportunities.

Credentialing

The previously discussed small education-focused programs provide funding or assist transitioning service members and veterans in applying for and remaining in school. The following programs have a more direct link to the civilian labor market by identifying how military skills give participants a head start in pursuing specific civilian career paths:

- DoD's **Credentialing Opportunities Online** (COOL) portal defies easy categorization because it helps transitioning service members earn credits (academic or otherwise) for skills that they gained in the military. Each military branch has its own COOL portal that allows users to find certifications, licenses, or exams that match their skills. Credentialing assistance can include funding, but the combined expenses for credentialing and tuition assistance cannot exceed $4,000 (see Army COOL, 2024).
- DOL's **United States Military Apprenticeship Program** is similar to COOL in that it empowers active-duty service members to gain formal recognition for the employable skills that they gained through their military service. Service members can log the hours that they have worked in a trade during their time in the military. The program also provides accreditation and free training in those trades.

Employment-Focused Programs

The landscape of small federal programs that provide employment support to transitioning service members and veterans is varied. Some focus on helping them find specific jobs (or even providing these jobs), while others assist more broadly by providing job-search assistance or helping them develop the skills associated with successful employment.

The SBA is involved in the military-to-civilian transition process mostly through entrepreneurship trainings. Although the TAP makes a distinction between employment and entrepreneurship, we group these programs with other employment services because of the significant overlap in their focus on preparing transitioning service members and veterans for the civilian labor market. Generally, searching for programs administered by the SBA is a good way to find federally funded entrepreneurship training opportunities.

Business Skills

We group the following SBA programs together under "business skills" because they focus on business management, which could apply to both self-employment and traditional employment, including managerial jobs:

- The SBA's **Veterans Business Outreach Center** program provides entrepreneurial training to service members, veterans, and their family members. These services can be extremely broad, such as "assistance and training in such areas as international trade, franchising, internet marketing, accounting, and more" (SBA, 2024b). Program centers are physical locations and are funded by federal grants. These locations also host workshops and activities for other programs, including the other programs in this category.

- The SBA's **Boots to Business** (B2B) training workshop functions primarily as an optional component of the TAP; its **B2B Reboot** program offers similar classes post-transition, and its online **B2B Revenue Readiness** course helps veterans continue studying financial planning for businesses.
- The **Veteran Federal Procurement Entrepreneur Training Program**, which is also funded by the SBA, provides grants to businesses owned by veterans.

The SBA also provides funding for specialized trainings for specific transitioning populations, including military spouses, Native Americans, women, and service-disabled veterans (SBA, 2024a). The following SBA programs fund online and in-person training sessions across the country:

- The **Women Veteran Entrepreneurship Training Program** offers training, advising services, loans, and connections to federal contract opportunities to female veterans who are seeking to start or expand a small business.
- The **Service-Disabled Veteran Entrepreneurship Training Program** provides entrepreneurship training, mentorship, and networking opportunities to veterans with a service-connected disability.

Job-Search Assistance

As we discuss in earlier chapters, job-search assistance is a common feature of many employment-focused transition programs. However, it is possible that smaller programs are organized to provide more-individualized assistance or to serve veterans who face specific types of barriers to traditional employment. A detailed assessment of the effectiveness of these programs could provide insights for all programs with job-search assistance components by both improving an understanding of the needs of veteran jobseekers and identifying the types of challenges that they encounter in searching for civilian employment opportunities or retaining employment while serving in the reserves. The following programs focus on job-search assistance:

- DoD's **Education and Employment Initiative** helps wounded, ill, or injured service members find jobs that can accommodate their disabilities. Program coordinators build relationships with employers and provide customized employment or education opportunities for service members.
- The Office of Personnel Management's **Vets to Feds** program helps veterans find federal jobs and assists with the application process.
- DoD's **Employer Support of the Guard and Reserve** acts as a go-between for National Guard or reserve service members and their civilian employers, assisting with com-

munication and resolving conflicts associated with military members' transitions to the employment aspect of postservice life. The program's primary purpose is to recognize employers that have hired reserve-component service members and ensure compliance with the Uniformed Services Employment and Reemployment Rights Act of 1994 (Pub. L. 103-353, 1994).

- DOL's **Homeless Veterans' Reintegration Program** provides grants to organizations that offer employment-focused counseling to homeless veterans. Job-search service providers that receive grants through this program can offer other benefits, including job placement and housing assistance.

Job Matching and On-the-Job Training

We have discussed organizations that help veterans find jobs, but a significant number of federal programs connect transitioning service members to employment opportunities by hiring them directly, including the following:

- DoD's **Operation Warfighter** program finds jobs for transitioning service members at medical facilities and connects them with the relevant hiring offices, supervisors, and mentors. Although the program is intended to be used on a temporary basis, the skills that veterans gain and the contacts that they make could open doors to long-term employment opportunities.
- VA's **Compensated Work Therapy** program supports veterans with physical and mental health challenges by organizing vocational rehabilitation partnerships with participating employers, which might improve these veterans' long-term career prospects.
- VA's **Warrior Training Advancement Course** similarly targets wounded transitioning service members by preparing them for specific jobs in VA, either as a veteran service representative or a rating veteran service representative. VA also offers nonveteran-specific training for other VA positions that are available to transitioning service members (VA, 2024b).
- The **VA Veterans Work-Study Program** provides immediate part-time jobs to student veterans. VA provides beneficiaries with a minimum wage, advance pay (if needed), and a job at a higher-education institution, VA facility, state agency, or other federal or state non-VA organization.
- VA's **Warriors to Workforce** program has an expanded mission and trains wounded veterans for federal contracting jobs.
- DoD's **SkillBridge** internship program partners with businesses to provide active-duty service members with work experience in the six months before their separation date. These service members use paid military time to actively develop employment skills and forge connections in an industry that can lead to long-term employment immediately after they leave the military.

Sector-Specific Employment Support

There are many small federal programs that provide employment or internship opportunities beyond VA, including the following:

- The **Veterans Innovation Partnership Fellowship** program is directly funded by the U.S. Department of State. Veterans serve a yearlong internship with a federal foreign affairs agency, although it is limited to those with a relevant master's degree. The internship is intended to provide experience and exposure that prepare veterans for careers in diplomacy, international development, and related fields.
- The U.S. Department of Energy's **Federal Energy Management Program's Scholars Program** provides paid internship opportunities to both veterans and nonveterans, including housing and commuting allowances.
- DoD's **Troops to Teachers** program is intended to help transitioning service members and veterans become teachers. The program was reauthorized in December 2021 after being canceled in October 2020, but it did not receive a restart fund and is offered only in some states (Defense Activity for Non-Traditional Education Support, undated).
- The **Veteran Registered Nurses in Primary Care Training Program** is one example of a small program funded by the U.S. Department of Health and Human Services. It is dedicated to assisting veterans who are interested in becoming nurses.
- The USDA's **Enhancing Agricultural Opportunities for Military Veterans** program, which is popularly known as "AgVets," provides grants to organizations that expose veterans to farmwork experience, noting that although "military veterans are eligible for most USDA programs, a hands-on immersive training experience has been identified as a critical strategy for helping interested individuals enter into and sustain successful careers" (USDA, undated). This sentiment seems to be shared by most of the organizations in this chapter.

Transition Programs for Nonveterans

Some programs identified as assisting with military transitions do not actually target transitioning service members and veterans themselves. Many counseling programs, such as the TAP and DoD's Yellow Ribbon Reintegration Program, provide benefits to dependents of transitioning service members and veterans, but some programs go farther, focusing exclusively on families. We discuss the largest such program, DEA, in Chapter 2. However, there are also much smaller programs with similar missions, including the following:

- DoD's **Spouse Education and Career Opportunities** offers both broad and targeted career counseling, as well as job- and education-search assistance for the spouses of transitioning service members and veterans.

- ED's **Iraq and Afghanistan Service Grant** is a benefit specifically reserved for dependents of service members who died as a result of service in Iraq or Afghanistan.
- An example of a service-level initiative is the U.S. Coast Guard's **Spouse Employment Assistance Program**, which offers counseling on career planning, job searching, and the job application process.

Conclusions

Clearly, there is a massive variety of small transition programs competing and cooperating to accomplish interacting, overlapping, and supporting goals. Our review was limited to a high-level assessment of program goals, activities, and areas of redundancy and overlap. A dedicated full-scale analysis of small-program uptake, alongside a comprehensive outcome-oriented evaluation of all federally funded transition programs, would provide more insights into how these programs use their resources to support transitioning service members and veterans and how effective they have been in doing so.

CHAPTER 6

Content Analysis of the 45 Federal Transition Programs

Since September 11, 2001, federal programs to assist veterans in transitioning to civilian life have increased in number across various agencies. GAO has conducted several analyses of federal transition programs, including their features and performance. However, there is little evidence of effectiveness at both ends of the program-size spectrum. In this chapter, we present findings from our analysis of 45 transition programs, using legislation, program descriptions, and existing literature about the programs as data inputs. Our novel approach involves analyzing program participation relative to program cost and showing which transition programs consume outsized levels of funding relative to their reach.

Overview of GAO's Findings and Study Limitations

GAO identified 45 federally funded transition programs operating in FY 2017 that facilitated military-to-civilian employment transitions for service members, veterans, and their families and that are overseen by a total of 11 U.S. government agencies (GAO, 2019a; GAO, 2020). GAO found a great deal of overlap in the activities and goals of these programs, as well as variation in their budgets and the extent to which the agencies evaluated the effectiveness of their programs. Nine of the 45 programs had neither tracked their outcomes nor conducted any type of evaluation. GAO's congressionally mandated analysis examined

> (1) the extent to which the programs provide similar services to similar populations, and how agencies coordinate to manage any duplication, overlap, or fragmentation; and
> (2) what federal agencies have done to assess the effectiveness of programs to help service-members achieve civilian employment (GAO, 2020, p. 2).

The federal government dedicates billions of dollars each year to military-to-civilian employment transitions, and GAO found that three large programs receive the vast majority of this funding: the PGIB, VR&E, and DEA.

GAO reports provide the most comprehensive picture of federal transition programs to date but have their limitations. The 2020 report and other reports that focus on narrower transition-related topics have documented only a limited set of program features and characteristics, such as the number of participants, the agency managing the program, and program budget levels. Documenting additional program features would better illustrate the variety of transition programs and services available through the federal government. Furthermore, GAO data on federal transition programs came from self-reported information by program representatives. It is unclear how respondents to GAO solicitations interpreted data requests or whether they reported their respective budgets and program participants consistently. Some budget data appear to be inconsistent with figures reported in other reports. For example, the 2020 GAO report indicated that the VR&E budget was $231.5 million in FY 2017, whereas VBA's FY 2022 annual budget report lists expenditures as $1.47 billion (GAO, 2020, p. 25; VBA, 2023a, p. 244).

We have attempted to compile our own updated budget and expenditure data for all 45 identified programs, but we could not find consistent information for a subset of these programs. This missing information is a significant shortfall of government reporting of veteran transition program funding and performance. There is no single source that provides consistent and reliable budgetary reporting for these programs in the U.S. government. Occasionally, a single report, such as the 2020 GAO report, has reported wildly different budgetary figures for a single program across FYs with no explanation for the change.

Taxonomy for Additional Program Features

Although we were not able to collect an updated set of program participant and budget figures that was more comprehensive and more consistent than those reported by GAO, we did identify additional features of these 45 federal transition programs that can enhance understanding of the variety of federal programs that support veterans' transitions. We reviewed program websites and other official, publicly available program materials and coded each of these features.

Unlike GAO, we did not solicit this information directly from program officials. In an earlier stage of this research, we reached out to representatives from each of these federal programs to complete a survey or interview them. However, no program officials responded to our survey, and very few agreed to an interview. The lack of willingness by program officials to provide the information requested in the initial stages of this research project is concerning from a transparency standpoint, and it raises questions about the responsiveness of the agencies charged with managing and overseeing these programs.

Table 6.1 lists the additional program characteristics we coded, along with a short description of the measure and the coding scheme that we used to classify the 45 programs according to each characteristic.

TABLE 6.1

Federal Transition Program Feature Taxonomy Codes

Program Characteristic	Definition	Coding
RECIPIENT of funds	Who receives government funds?	1: Beneficiary (direct payment) 2: A program or provider on behalf of beneficiary (e.g., tuition payment) 3: Organization under grant or contract to provide services to beneficiary 4: Pay for labor as intern, fellow, or worker 5: Unpaid work or intern opportunity 6: Government office or staff 7: Both individual and program or provider
AGENCY providing funds	Who is providing government funds?	List agency
OVERSIGHT by Congress	Which congressional committee has oversight responsibility for the program?	List committee
TRAINING OPPORTUNITY provided	Is this a specific or general training/education opportunity or program?	0: Advice, coordination, navigation, or counseling, but not training 1: General education or training (participant's choice) 2: Higher education only 3: Specific skill training limitation
TIMING of program	When is the program available and used?	1: Any time preseparation 2: Immediately before separation (including requirement to begin program 180 days out) 3: Transition period, including after separation (+/– 12 months) 4: Postservice and veterans only 5: Lifetime eligibility 6: Unclear time restriction
LOCATION of services	Where is the program accessed?	1: On base 2: Off but near base 3: Major metropolitan area 4: Online 5: College campus 6: Unclear 5: Other
APPROVAL to participate	Does the person need approval to participate?	0: Eligibility check only 1: Yes, chain of command approval is needed (active duty) 2: Yes, participation is approved by program provider 3: Unclear
ENTITLEMENT to participate	Is the program universal or limited by special criteria?	1: Universal or near-universal entitlement 2: Limiting criteria

Table 6.1—Continued

Program Characteristic	Definition	Coding
SPECIAL POPULATION served by program	What special population served by the program?	0: Transitioning service members and veterans 1: All transitioning service members 2: All veterans 3: All dependents (spouses and children) 4: High-risk transitioning service members or veterans 5: Reserve component 6: Wounded, ill, or injured veteran and their survivors 7: Military occupational specialty 8: Desired industry or occupation 9: Demographic minority population 10: Other
BENEFIT is monetary provided directly or for in-kind services	Is the benefit provided to the transitioning service member or veteran monetary or in-kind services?	1: Direct cash payment (not employment pay) 2: Payment to entity on behalf of participant (e.g., for tuition, registration fees, exam costs) 3: In-kind service (e.g., mentoring, job fair) 4: Job or internship experience (paid or unpaid) 5: Other
LEVEL of program—individual or group	Is the program offered at the group or individual level?	1: Universal 2: Group, large 3: Group, small 4: Individual or one-on-one 5: Unclear
COSTS—direct only or additional significant hidden costs	Are there only direct monetary costs or also implied costs?	1: Direct costs to participate, including program or office overhead costs 2: Implied/hidden costs (e.g., missed workdays) 1+2 (3): Both direct and indirect costs
SCHEDULING—on or off duty time	Is the program accessed while on or off duty?	1: During duty time (active duty) 2: Off-duty time (active duty) 3: Duty becomes job or internship 4: N/A (dependent program) 5: Post-transition 6: Unclear
DELIVERY—self-guided, online, in-person, or hybrid	What is the mechanism for program participation?	1: Self-guided 2: Online 3: In-person 4: Hybrid, mix of online and in person 5: Unclear

Data Collection

To collect program data, we searched the internet using the program names to identify any official government websites or documents. We did not expand beyond official government materials to ensure that the types of materials that we collected for all programs were consistent, regardless of their size, budget, or level of public scrutiny. The exception to this approach was in identifying program budget information. We used all available resources to identify program budget and cost information, especially for the largest programs serving transitioning veterans. We were not able to find comparable budget data for all the programs in the GAO report.

Weighting

We did not identify any additional official federal programs implemented in the time since the 2020 GAO report on the initial 45 federal programs. There are some programs that are being piloted or tested, such as the ENPP, but because of the limited information available at the time of our research, we opted to exclude them from this analysis. GAO's definition of *career assistance programs* includes those serving dependents, such as the children and spouses of service members, under the logic that the entire family transitions out of the military and that the transition outcomes of a military spouse will have consequences for the entire family, including the veteran.

Our coding process recorded characteristics of the programs, but the programs varied dramatically in scale and scope, as indicated by budget size and number of program participants, among other factors. For this reason, we analyzed program feature information in multiple ways. First, we considered the characteristics at the program level, treating each program with equal weight. We also weighted program features using two kinds of weights—budget and number of participants—and summarized the weighted data. Weighting by program budget levels revealed the distribution of program features based on costs or spending. Weighting by number of participants showed us the distribution of program features based on how many participants potentially experienced them. Hypothetically, if there were a comparable number of programs focused on higher education and postmilitary employment, but the budget for education programs was higher by an order of magnitude, we might question whether there was an opportunity to improve funding for postmilitary employment programs. The budget- and participant-weighted analyses helped us identify potential gaps in the availability of programs serving specific populations or transition needs and where there might be opportunities to better align the budgets of federal transition programs with their levels of participation.

Results

Table 6.2 lists the top ten programs in terms of budget. For its 2020 report, GAO solicited budget information from the programs themselves, and not all programs reported back. GAO calculated each program's relative share of federal employment transition dollars using only these reported budgets. We attempted to collect updated budget information for all the programs. However, we could not find these data for all programs, and what we could collect came from various years between 2019 and 2023. We report the budget data we compiled for comparison, but the lack of completeness makes the RAND-identified figures less useful

TABLE 6.2

Top Ten Largest Federal Transition Programs, by Budget Level

Program	Relative % of Budget from GAO Report	Relative % of Budget Identified by RAND	GAO Reported Budget in FY 2017 ($)
PGIB (or Chapter 33)	84.05	84.12	11,056,959,000
DEA	4.2	8.42	553,128,000
DoD's Tuition Assistance Program	3.46	1.43	455,656,053
All-Volunteer Force Educational Assistance (or MGIB) – Active Duty	2.27		298,818,000
VR&E	1.76	0.23	231,472,000[a]
JVSG	1.33		174,895,912
All-Volunteer Force Educational Assistance (or MGIB) – Selected Reserve	0.99	1.18	130,311,000
Compensated Work Therapy	0.46	0.23	61,069,433
VA Work-Study Program	0.37		48,295,632
Homeless Veterans' Reintegration Program	0.34	0.45	44,929,908

SOURCES: Features data from GAO, 2019a; GAO, 2020.

NOTE: The only consistently reported budget information on all 45 programs comes from GAO, 2020, Appendix II, Table 6.

[a] Highlights a dramatic increase from FY 2017 to FY 2018.

in calculating budget weights. Because the budget information from GAO reports was more complete, we used those data to create the budget weights, or the proportion of total federal employment transition funding spent on each program.

The PGIB has, by far, the largest budget of any of the 45 transition programs and is more than an order of magnitude larger than the next largest program. The PGIB provides educational benefits for service members, veterans, and (in some cases) dependents, and it accounts for almost 85 percent of all spending on federal transition programs. Of the top ten programs by budget, six provided direct payments for education benefits to service members, veterans, and dependents. Four provided some employment resources or assistance. Notably, the TAP, which is mandatory for all transitioning service members, does not appear on the list. This might be because of a lack of clarity in the submitted budget that GAO used for its report. It might be that only the operating budget for the Military-Civilian Transition Office, which oversees the TAP, and its personnel was included and not the additional expense of the TAP contractors who teach the curriculum on bases. It certainly does not include the implicit cost of taking approximately 200,000 transitioning service members off duty for three to five days to complete the program. It is clear that most federal funds allocated to veteran transition programs emphasize education over immediate employment. Of the top ten, seven provide education benefits. Only JVSG is primarily an employment program, although VR&E's purpose is to help veterans become employable.

Budgets are not the only way to measure program size and results. We also order the programs by the number of participants that GAO reported to have used each program, presented in Table 6.3. As with the budget figures, these figures were reported to GAO by the programs themselves.

Once again, the PGIB tops the list, serving more than 655,000 people—nearly three times as many participants as the next largest program. Other top programs by participant number include large education benefit programs, as well as DoD's Employer Support of the Guard and Reserve, DoD's Transition Assistance Advisors, and military spouse employment programs. Although employment-focused programs are not well represented among the most *expensive* federal transition programs, they do serve a relatively large number of people.

We identified 14 features of transition programs and coded each program as described earlier. Table 6.4 reports the distribution of program features at the program level. We also computed the distribution of program features weighted by reported participants and by program budget. The latter provides insight into which features participants experience relatively more or less than others, as well as the policy implications of various program features,

TABLE 6.3

Top Ten Federal Transition Programs, by Number of Participants

Program	Relative % Served	Number Served
PGIB (or Chapter 33)	24.52	655,430
DoD's Tuition Assistance Program	8.77	234,456
Employer Support of the Guard and Reserve	7.85	209,927
TAP	7.45	199,218
Transition Assistance Advisors	7.41	198,198
Spouse Education and Career Opportunities	6.73	180,000
Military OneSource Spouse Career Center	6.17	165,000
VR&E	4.95	132,218
JVSG	4.63	123,869
DEA	3.75	100,275

SOURCES: Features data from GAO, 2019a; GAO, 2020.

TABLE 6.4

Distribution of Program Characteristics Under Various Weighting Strategies

Characteristic	Program Weight	Participant Weight	Budget Weight
Recipient (number of programs)	44	40	35
Beneficiary cash	2.27	0.00	0.00
Program on behalf of beneficiary	20.45	17.01	0.00
Grant or contract for services to beneficiary	34.09	16.27	11.19
Pay for labor	13.64	2.88	2.07
Unpaid internship	2.27	0.02	0.83
Government office or staff	22.73	34.35	0.10
Both individual and program receives funds	4.55	29.47	85.81
Agency (number of programs)	45	40	35
USDA	2.22	0.00	0.04
U.S. Department of Homeland Security	6.67	2.62	0.07
U.S. Department of Energy	2.22	0.00	0.00
DOL	4.44	5.24	1.67
DoD	28.89	48.88	3.72
ED	6.67	0.31	0.18
U.S. Department of Health and Human Services	2.22	0.04	0.07
U.S. Office of Personnel Management	2.22	0.00	0.00
SBA	11.11	1.51	0.05
U.S. Department of State	2.22	0.00	0.00
U.S. Department of the Treasury	2.22	0.00	94.19
VA	28.89	41.4	0.04
Type of training (number of programs)	45	40	35
Curriculum or training on transition only	2.22	7.45	0.03
On-the-job training or internship	11.11	5.44	2.13
General training or education	20.00	41.00	95.14
Specific skill or occupation training or education	35.56	9.95	2.07
Advising or counseling through a specific office	28.89	36.16	0.63
Website or self-directed resource	2.22	0.00	0.00

Table 6.4—Continued

Characteristic	Program Weight	Participant Weight	Budget Weight
Timing (number of programs)	45	40	35
Anytime preseparation	22.22	28.47	4.71
Immediately prior to separation	13.33	15.18	0.09
Transition period, including after separation	8.89	5.33	1.82
Post-service or veterans only	40.00	16.07	7.00
Lifetime eligibility	8.89	27.1	86.36
Unclear time restriction	6.67	7.85	0.01
Location (number of programs)	44	40	35
On base	4.55	3.63	0.00
On and off base (nearby)	2.27	0.02	0.00
On base and online	11.36	9.62	0.04
Off base (nearby) or unclear	2.27	0.22	0.00
Major metropolitan area	13.64	1.89	0.39
Online	6.82	20.32	0.05
College campus	31.82	43.14	95.27
Other	27.27	21.15	4.24
Approval (number of programs)	45	40	35
Eligibility check	33.33	61.63	87.49
Chain of command	11.11	7.76	0.04
Program provider	55.56	30.61	12.47
Entitlement (number of programs)	45	40	35
Universal or near-universal entitlement	26.67	47.89	91.32
Limited criteria or special population	73.33	52.11	8.68
Special populations (number of programs)	45	40	35
Transitioning service members and veterans	8.89	28.25	87.33
All transitioning service members	13.33	17.01	3.60
All dependents (spouses and children)	6.67	12.92	0.00
High-risk transitioning service members and veterans	8.89	5.56	1.81
Reserve component	8.89	15.33	0.15

Table 6.4—Continued

Characteristic	Program Weight	Participant Weight	Budget Weight
Wounded, ill, or injured service members or veterans and their dependents	15.56	11.19	6.43
Military occupational specialty	4.44	4.11	0.10
Desired industry or occupation	13.33	0.05	0.12
Demographic minority population	2.22	0.20	0.00
Other	17.78	5.38	0.45
Benefit (number of programs)	45	40	35
Direct cash payment	15.56	29.71	86.18
Payment to entity on behalf of participant	20.00	16.28	7.79
In-kind service (e.g., mentoring, job fair)	46.67	32.47	0.50
Job or internship experience	17.78	21.54	5.53
Level (number of programs)	44	39	34
Universal	2.27	7.45	0.03
Group, large	4.55	7.86	0.01
Group, small	4.55	0.02	0.00
Individual or one-on-one	81.82	82.53	99.88
Unclear	6.82	2.13	0.07
Costs (number of programs)	45	40	35
Direct costs to participate, including program overhead	86.67	0.00	99.96
Implied or hidden costs (e.g., missed workdays)	2.22	92.24	0.00
Both direct and indirect costs	11.11	7.76	0.04
Scheduling (number of programs)	45	40	35
During duty time (active duty)	6.67	11.05	0.04
Off-duty time (active duty)	13.33	17.27	3.76
Duty becomes job or internship	6.67	0.29	0.00
Dependent program	11.11	16.67	4.21
Post-transition	60.00	46.87	91.99
Unclear	2.22	7.85	0.01

Table 6.4—Continued

Characteristic	Program Weight	Participant Weight	Budget Weight
Delivery (number of programs)	45	40	35
Self-guided	4.44	0.53	0.1
Online	6.67	20.32	0.05
In-person	35.56	6.9	1.01
Hybrid of delivery methods	42.22	64.55	97.43
Unclear	11.11	7.7	1.41

NOTE: No budget information was available for several programs, including those serving exclusively spouses and children. For this reason, the number of programs is lower (e.g., 35 versus 45), and there is no calculated budget weight because there was no budget information about this special population.

according to their relative proportion of the budget. As noted, treating all programs equally skews an analysis of program features because of the handful of very large, very expensive programs and many smaller, more-limited programs. We note the sample sizes for each column because applying the participant and budget weights means that some programs drop out because of unreported budgets or participant numbers.

Federal transition programs offer many different types of benefits to participants, such as direct cash payments, basic online trainings, and informational websites. We code for the primary way that program resources were used to assist transitioning individuals. At the program level, few programs (2.3 percent) provide payments directly to beneficiaries. Most use their resources to pay another entity for services: Just over 20 percent of the programs support payment directly to an organization for services provided on behalf of individual beneficiaries, around one-third (34.1 percent) fund a contract to provide services, and around one-fifth use their funds primarily to staff a government office that provides transition services. When weighting by program participants, the relative balance shifts, driven primarily by the PGIB, which provides direct payments to participants and pays tuition fees to another entity (colleges or approved training programs), serves the largest number of participants, and has the largest budget.

The majority of federal transition programs are related to general education and training or specific industry or occupational skill-focused education or training. For example, under the category "Type of training," more than 55 percent of all programs provide education or training, and seven of the top ten by budget level provide education or training (see Table 6.2). According to the 2020 GAO report, more than 95 percent of total transition program dollars went to education programs, but just under 50 percent of participants enrolled in education or training programs. These participant-versus-budget–weighted program metrics suggest that these education and training programs consume a disproportionate share of funding relative to the number of participants that they serve.

Several other program features are shaped by the predominance of education-focused transition programs. For example, almost one-third of programs are offered on a college campus. Weighted by number of participants, more than 40 percent of all transition program participants are served by transition programs operating on college campuses, but these programs account for 95 percent of budget dollars. Because we code college classes as one-on-one or individual training, these education-focused transition programs mean that most programs, participants, and budget dollars for transition go to one-on-one or individual programs. Most education programs are also pursued postseparation, leading to most transition programs and budget dollars being used after separation from the military.

Federal transition programs are available at different points in the transition life cycle. Twenty-two percent of programs offer a benefit available any time before military separation, such as DoD's Tuition Assistance Program and Military Apprenticeship Program. Forty percent are available to individuals only after separation, and just under 10 percent are available across the military life cycle, meaning that they can be used before or after separating from service. The relative distribution changed when weighting by participants and budgets, in large part because of the influence of the PGIB, which can be used before or after separation. There has been an interest in moving the planning and preparation for transition "to the left," or having service members begin the transition planning process earlier in advance of separation. Many programs exist that serve only individuals who have already separated (40 percent), but those programs appear to serve relatively fewer participants and cost relatively little because of the declining representation of postservice-only programs in the participant- and budget-weighted estimates.

Transition programs are offered across a wide variety of locations (e.g., on a military installation, off but near the installation, only in major metropolitan areas). Program location might present a barrier to access for some individuals if programs are located only on base or in a major metropolitan area. Nearly one-third of transition programs are offered on a college campus because such programs provide education benefits. However, there is a reasonable variety of locations where transition programs are offered. In terms of the number of participants they support, online programs predominate after programs on college campuses, which is largely an effect of the Military OneSource Spouse Career Center that serves a large number of military spouses. Because of the distribution of programs across locations includes online offerings, it does not appear that program site presents a major barrier to accessing programs and services.

Access to transition programs can be nearly universal or require application and approval by various gatekeepers, including one's chain of command (if still serving) or the agency offering the program, according to some known or unclear eligibility criteria. We code for who needed to approve program participation (if anyone), whether there were eligibility criteria that would limit access to program participation, and what those eligibility criteria were. Just over 10 percent of programs require their chain of command to approve participation, such as SkillBridge. Programs requiring chain of command approval run the risk of having a local commander make decisions about approval according to unit training needs or personal bias rather than the interest of the transitioning service member.[1] The majority of programs (56 percent) require some kind of approval for participation by the program offerer, which involves an application process that might be more or less competitive. Relatedly, 73 percent of programs have some kind of limit on eligibility, such as being intended for a special population, which is most often for those who were wounded, ill, or injured during service (16 percent of programs), those from a specific military occupation or pursuing a specific industry or occupation postservice (4 percent and 13 percent, respectively), those from the reserves (9 percent), and those who are understood to be at high risk (9 percent). The influence of the college-benefits programs is apparent in the participant- and budget-weighted results; these programs require only an eligibility check to be used because they are nearly universal entitlements available to virtually all service members and veterans.

Programs offer participants different benefits, such as providing cash payments directly to the participant, paying a fee to another entity on behalf of the participant, providing an in-kind service, or setting up an internship or work opportunity. Almost half (47 percent) of federal programs primarily provide a service to participants, 16 percent provide direct cash payment, 20 percent pay another entity on behalf of a participant, and 18 percent provide job or internship experiences. The influence of PGIB is again clear when considering the budget-weighted results, which indicate that 86 percent of transition programs' budget resources are spent on programs that provide direct cash payments to beneficiaries.

Programs predominately serve people at the individual level. Although the TAP involves attending classes together with others, the majority of programs actually serve people at the individual level, including college and education programs, internship programs, and vocational rehabilitation.

Because some programs involve active-duty individuals participating in the program instead of their normal duty, we code for whether programs had any implicit or hidden costs, whether they involved only direct program costs, or both. Indirect or hidden costs are any costs born from paying the salary or wages of an individual but not having them available to do their official duty. The TAP, which requires participants to spend three to five days in transition-assistance classes, would be one example. SkillBridge, which allows an approved service member to spend up to six months in a civilian internship while being paid by the military, is another example of programs with implicit costs. The participant-weighted results change dramatically because of the single program that provides tax exclusions for PGIB benefits. This program is entirely an implicit cost because of the lost tax revenues. But, the program has no budget amount and thus does not show up in the budget-weighted results. Although the number of programs that involve implicit costs is not large, it is worth noting that TAP serves close to 200,000 participants (GAO, 2020). Thus, the actual total implied costs of the TAP are likely to be very large. Similarly, the loss of a service member to a civil-

---

[1] According to anecdotal evidence from subject-matter experts, there have been leadership complaints about "short-timers" who use these programs "excessively" because the commanders could not prevent them from doing so.

ian employer for up to six months through the SkillBridge program has the potential to incur a tremendous amount of implied costs if the program serves more than a handful of service members.

Most federal transition programs are scheduled after individuals transition out of the military (60 percent). Approximately 20 percent are offered during active-duty time, including while on or off duty (7 percent and 13 percent, respectively). Eleven percent of programs are for dependents, and 7 percent provide a job or internship.

Federal programs are a mix of online and in-person activities: 35 percent of programs are in-person only, 42 percent are a mix of online and offline activities, and 7 percent are entirely online. The relative distribution shifts with the participant- and budget-weighted results to the extent that there is a greater representation of hybrid activities; this, again, is largely driven by the PGIB and MGIB, which allow for hybrid or online education.

Program Redundancies and Gaps

Both GAO and our study found that a small fraction of programs receive the vast majority of federal employment transition-assistance funding. For example, GAO found that in FY 2017, the PGIB, DEA, and DoD's Tuition Assistance Program were all employment-assistance programs despite their education-focused components. These programs accounted for 92 percent of an estimated $13.15 billion in federal funding that went toward helping service members, veterans, and their families transition to civilian employment in FY 2017. We note that VR&E's budget increased from $231 million in FY 2017 to $1.43 billion in FY 2018, according to the 2020 GAO report, although this might reflect a data error. Nonetheless, it is clear that the largest programs' budgets can fluctuate from year to year.

However, this does not change the fact that a small number of programs command the bulk of federal spending on transition, and that nearly all the money spent on *career assistance programs*, as defined by GAO, goes to upskilling, retraining, or education that can take many months or years to complete (GAO, 2020). Specifically, the 2020 GAO report found that 35 out of the 45 reviewed programs provided educational assistance. Of the largest federal programs, VR&E does offer some career counseling and long-term support for disabled veterans who wish to start their own businesses, but a large share of the program's budget is dedicated to vocational training and educational benefits.

GAO's analysis went even further to show redundancies specifically within this education component. GAO looked at programs that offered educational counseling and found that, for service members, veterans, spouses, and dependents, there are a total of 25 separate programs providing those services. Similarly, there are 21 programs that provide educational needs assessments. For comparison, there are 32 different programs that provide employment assistance, 22 of which provide employment counseling and résumé assistance.

Most striking are the number of programs that provided referrals for different services or resources: 22 *separate* referral programs for education, 23 programs for employment, and

17 programs for self-employment assistance. The 2020 GAO report did not assess the amount of confusion caused by the current set of transition programs. There is an entire industry dedicated to providing advice, guidance, and counseling to transitioning service members to help them navigate these transition programs. VA spends an entire day of the TAP educating service members about the benefit programs to which they are entitled and how to apply for benefits. These multiple redundancies should be eliminated with the goal of making the entire transition landscape less complex and easier to navigate. We note that there are 27 different programs that had limited to no budget information, that serve few transitioning service members or veterans, and that have no track record of performance. Shuttering these programs would be a good place to begin simplifying the transition landscape.

A major gap across the 45 programs is individualized employment assistance. Among programs that specifically provide employment assistance, that support was most often in the form of career assessments to help participants identify a civilian career field, referrals to veteran-friendly employers, résumé and cover letter writing assistance, and other forms of support that did not include job-specific skill development opportunities. Transitioning service members might be particularly well-served by developing the skills necessary to discern between high-quality training programs and lower-quality ones. VR&E provides a considerable amount of one-on-one counseling because of the specialized needs of that particular population. Furthermore, the ENPP will provide some one-on-one career counseling, although the extent is unclear; individual career counselors might provide career development services directly or guide veterans to resources in their community.

Transitioning service members often struggle to translate the skills that they have developed in their military occupations to civilian career opportunities. MyNextMove for Veterans is a DOL platform that attempts to address this need by matching military occupations and military-acquired skills with civilian occupations. However, prior analysis using data collected from service members suggest that MyNextMove's matches are typically not very highly related to a service member's military occupation, and, perhaps worse, MyNextMove often fails to recommend occupations that are closely related (Wenger, Pint, et al., 2017; Wenger, Roer, and Wong, 2023). RAND research has helped expand the list of civilian occupations that are recommended by MyNextMove to enlisted Army veterans. RAND researchers have also extended this functionality to the Navy, Marine Corps, and Air Force, but there are currently no plans to do so for the Space Force or Coast Guard. Although MyNextMove for Veterans does purport to crosswalk specific military occupational specialties to civilian careers, that is the extent of its personalized guidance. Otherwise, the platform functions similarly to other job search portals by allowing jobseekers to search for jobs by keyword and browse careers by occupation.

DoD's SkillBridge program provides apprenticeship opportunities and connects transitioning service members directly with participating employers. However, service members complete their SkillBridge apprenticeships in their last six months of duty, which takes them away from their units. The program is also limited by the number of participating employers. For these and other reasons, it is unlikely that such a program is scalable to serve larger numbers of participants. The ENPP, which is a DOL pilot program for TAP participants, appears to address the need for individualized career counseling, but evaluation results for the program have not been released.

Implications for Federal Transition Program Policy

There are important features of federal transition programs beyond how many people they serve and how much they cost that should be part of policy discussions about how best to meet the needs of transitioning military members.

First, the majority of federal transition programs focus on education. General education or specific occupational training are important ways to enhance the human capital of veterans and thus are expected to ultimately lead to enhanced employment outcomes after service. The PGIB is nearly universally available, provides extremely generous benefits, and accounts for the largest share of any program in the total budget for federal transition programs; it consumes 84 percent of all reported budget dollars for 45 programs. Even though the PGIB serves a large number of beneficiaries, it covers only 24 percent of all of the total beneficiaries served by all programs. This might make sense, because the PGIB is not only a transition program but also an important recruiting and retention tool. The overwhelming emphasis on education programs among federal transition programs means there are relatively fewer transition programs that focus on employment directly after service, and the reported budgets for those programs are much lower than the major education programs.

Employment-focused transition programs serve a larger share of program participants than their budget share. The four major short-term employment-assistance programs—the TAP, DoD's Transition Assistance Advisors, JVSG, and Employer Support of the Guard and Reserve—together account for 27 percent of federal program participants reported by GAO, yet these programs collectively report to have only 1.4 percent of the federal transition program budget dollars. The TAP is the largest employment-focused transition program by number of participants, and it is now mandatory for transitioning active-duty and some reserve-component service members. As a result, the program is the subject of a great deal of scrutiny from veterans, lawmakers, and the general public. JVSG is another large-scale employment program serving many veterans. Employer Support of the Guard and Reserve is a large employment program but is limited to the reserves. Other employment-focused federal transition programs tend to be relatively small (e.g., internship programs) or serve a specific population, such as spouses or disabled veterans. Employment-focused transition programs serve many participants, but they do so with a relatively small fraction of total federal funding for transition programs.

Second, efforts to shift the transition process to earlier in a service member's timeline imply the need for more programs that are available for use before separation or transition. The large, expensive education benefit programs are, in principle, available to service members before they separate from the military, but, for various reasons, they typically use their benefits after separation. Expanding opportunities to use these programs during military service—and particularly while on duty—can come with increased costs in terms of diverted time and attention from military responsibilities but might be considerably less expensive overall.

Third, there should be a full accounting of all costs associated with federal transition programs, including program budgets, contracts and expenditures to other entities, and the implicit costs from lost tax revenues or lost duty days.

Fourth, more than 70 percent of federal transition programs have some limitation and serve a specific population. For example, there are programs that target ill or injured service members and programs that connect participants with jobs in specific fields that are designed to align with a service member's military occupation or desired civilian occupation. In addition, others serve a particular group, such as high-risk transitioning service members or those from minority demographic groups. Transition programs that focus on specific industries or occupations are more common than programs targeting high-risk service members. If smaller programs and resources were to be consolidated, it would be prudent to invest in transition programs for service members at the greatest risk of unemployment, which would require having better procedures to identify at-risk individuals and building more and stronger programs to help them early in the military-to-civilian transition process.

CHAPTER 7

Conclusions and Recommendations

Separating from the military is a complicated process. Service members can separate at different points of their careers—some after three years, others after 30—and which careers they transition *to* can vary. Some return to school, some find a new employer, some retire altogether, and others might start a business. One common characteristic of these different career paths is that transitioning service members have many decisions to make. Should they pursue training and accreditation in a particular occupation, or is additional education in a college setting the better choice for them? Some service members might need career counseling, job-search assistance, and help translating their military skills into civilian jobs. Additionally, families also sacrifice employment opportunities and educational continuity to the demands of the service member's military career, and veterans might continue to depend on family members after leaving the military. For each possible postservice future for veterans and their families, the U.S. government likely offers a transition support program to facilitate it. However, as prior RAND research has shown, many veterans are unable to leverage their military skills in their civilian jobs (Wenger, Roer, and Wong, 2023; Wenger, Miller, et al., 2017).

The federal government spends billions of dollars each year on these programs, but there has been little analysis of how this funding is apportioned, how programs use their funding, where there is overlap in program activities, whether the most expensive programs serve a proportionate number of participants, and how effective the programs have been in improving participants' employment outcomes. GAO conducted a congressionally mandated assessment of federally funded programs that help transitioning service members, veterans, and their families acquire skills and education to prepare them for civilian employment (GAO, 2019a; GAO, 2020). In cataloguing 45 such programs that are overseen by 11 federal agencies, GAO found a great deal of overlap in their activities and goals. Since GAO conducted its study, we find that little has changed: The same 45 programs remain active, and with the exception of a few pilot programs, there have been no new additions to the employment transition landscape.

In this report, we extended and updated GAO's analysis by reviewing the literature on employment transition programs, assessing budgetary and policy documents, and determining how these federal transition programs function, whom they serve, how many people they serve, and what evidence is available to indicate how they perform.

To facilitate our analysis, we grouped the same 45 programs that GAO identified by the size of their budgets by dividing them into following four categories:

1. **Big Four budgetary programs:** the PGIB, VR&E, DoD's Tuition Assistance Program, and DEA
2. **second-tier programs:** the MGIB and JVSG
3. **third-tier program:** DoD's TAP
4. **small programs:** an assortment of additional programs with significantly smaller budgets and serving significantly smaller target populations than the other three categories of programs.

In Chapter 6, we analyzed the program data through multiple lenses—(1) weighting the programs by the size of the populations they served, (2) examining each program individually, and (3) weighting the programs by budget size.

Key Findings

Most Employment Transition Programs Are Actually Focused on Education

According to the 2020 GAO report, more than 95 percent of total transition program budget dollars went to education programs, but just under 50 percent of participants enrolled in education or training programs. These participant-versus-budget–weighted program metrics suggest that these education and training programs consume a disproportionate share of funding relative to the number of participants that they serve. These education programs, particularly the PGIB, provide large incentives to participate by covering a significant portion of costs for housing, tuition, and materials for attending school.

Overall, we found that very few programs—and a small amount of overall funding for military-to-civilian employment transitions—are dedicated specifically to helping service members and veterans translate their military skills to the civilian labor market, helping them to find civilian apprenticeships or jobs, or connecting them with civilian employers. Nearly all the money spent on *career assistance programs*, as defined by GAO, is spent on upskilling, retraining, or education that can take many months or years to complete. There are limited exceptions. Two standout programs are SkillBridge, which is an apprenticeship-like program in which service members work for a civilian business or other organization for up to six months at the end of their military service, and the ENPP, which is a DOL pilot program that provides one-on-one career assistance to transitioning service members at selected military installations.

Although education benefits make up an outsized portion of the overall federal transition program budget, those programs receive limited scrutiny. The budgetary Big Four programs—the PGIB, VR&E, DoD's Tuition Assistance Program, and DEA—accounted for

$13.5 billion in federal transition program spending in FY 2019 out of a total allocation of $14.3 billion, or 94 percent of the total expenditures on transition aid. The third-tier program TAP costs approximately $140 million and serves *all* transitioning service members. This program received slightly less than 1 percent of all federal funds dedicated to military-to-civilian transitions. Additionally, the program is under-resourced, and there is limited information about the service-specific occupational matches to the civilian sector.

There Is Limited Evidence That Federally Funded Employment Transition Programs Are Effective

One of our most important findings is that there is virtually no evidence that any of the programs we examined has had a direct effect on transition outcomes. In some cases, the evidence was counterintuitive: The large, interagency TAP, which is overseen by DoD, was associated with lower wages for those who participate in the program; similarly, the PGIB resulted in modest increases in education but limited effects on earnings—and, in some cases, negative returns on investment in schooling. Other programs had no reported data, evaluation plans, resources, or outcome measures. Perhaps as a result, there have been few evaluations of program effectiveness.

In the few such evaluations that exist, the results are telling. For example, one study used administrative data from the U.S. Army, VA, and National Student Clearinghouse and found that approximately 40 percent of eligible Army veterans use PGIB benefits, and there is particularly low usage among veterans who had held combat occupations in the Army—a demographic that would likely benefit the most from education and training in a field that is more easily translatable to the civilian labor market (Kofoed, 2020). Other research has shown that PGIB beneficiaries have lower wages relative to those who do not use the program (Barr et al., 2021). For the second-largest program, VR&E, which supports disabled veterans, GAO found only modest evidence of improved performance over time (GAO, 2014a). For example, GAO found that among the 17,000 veterans who participated in the program in FY 2003, about half had been placed in a suitable job by FY 2012 (GAO, 2014a). Other big-budget programs, such as the DEA and DoD's Tuition Assistance Program, are considered to be transition programs by GAO but are not oriented primarily toward service members' transitions.

Although it might seem difficult to effectively evaluate these programs, there are multiple examples of large federal programs that have undergone high-quality evaluations. Most of these examples include randomized controlled trials. Perhaps the most relevant example is the series of Workforce Innovation and Opportunity Act evaluations conducted by Mathematica Policy Research on behalf of DOL. One particularly relevant study randomly selected participants and nonparticipants to receive individualized staff assistance as part of a program similar to the ENPP (Rosenberg et al., 2015). The study showed significant increases in wages among participants. The study's design promoted strong internal and external validity and showed evidence of the program's effectiveness. Each federal transition program would have to develop appropriate outcome measures, but these measures would generally be obvious, such as completion of degree programs; employment outcomes, including hours and earnings; and business profitability. It is crucial to include either nonparticipants or a control group to overcome selection bias.

Transition Programs Face Limited Oversight and Budgetary Scrutiny

The largest program in terms of budget, the PGIB, provides little information on participation, i.e., how many service members and veterans use it. Overall, we found that oversight is weak across all 45 federal transition programs, which could be because such oversight is fragmented. Numerous congressional committees are responsible for overseeing portions of some programs, and numerous federal agencies are involved in operating these programs. For example, the TAP curriculum is delivered by multiple agencies, but DoD is ultimately responsible for oversight, implementation, and program access. This arrangement makes it complicated for House and Senate committees—other than the House and Senate Armed Services Committees—to require evaluations of the program or mandate changes to it. For example, the House and Senate Veterans Committees might want oversight because their constituents are the beneficiaries of many of the programs, but the committee members cannot influence veterans' access to or the implementation of many programs. Weak oversight also has implications for access to transition support. Service members at remote installations might find it much more difficult to access transition services. In-person courses and training are often unavailable, and online modules are less preferred and less effective at facilitating learning (Kofoed et al., 2021). Reserve component personnel whose duty assignments require them to attend the TAP might face difficulty in finding the time to complete the curriculum. It is important that the same opportunities are available to all service members who need employment-focused transition support.

Another symptom of this oversight challenge is that program redundancies are common. This is especially true for education-focused programs that provide multiple types of education counseling and support various other programs.

There Are Opportunities to Address Redundancies in the Transition Programs and Services

Finally, we found numerous redundancies in available transition programs and services. There are many specific occupational skill-focused training programs that serve relatively limited numbers of participants. There might be opportunities to consolidate multiple programs that provide on-the-job training in specific skill sets to improve outreach and to reduce overhead costs and duplications of effort. The involvement of various federal agencies can make such consolidation challenging, so this is an area in need of more research. In general, a relatively large number of transition programs serve a relatively small and limited population, and, without sufficient evaluation of the return on investment from these programs, it is difficult to identify which specific programs could be consolidated or discontinued to make resources available to others.

Recommendations

We found a great deal of inconsistency in how budgets were reported across even large transition-assistance programs, and we encountered few robust evaluations of program effectiveness in our review of the military-to-civilian employment transition landscape. Because the federal government spends an estimated $12 billion annually on education, training, and other aspects of military-to-civilian transitions, it is critical that the agencies receiving these funds are held accountable for consistently reporting how their program budgets are allocated and whom they have served. We encountered several challenges in finding reliable, updated budget numbers, which could be a result of shortfalls in oversight and variations in reporting requirements.

However, the most notable gap was the paucity of program evaluations. Although there have been congressionally mandated assessments of some programs, much of the information that we did find on program effectiveness came from small-scale or otherwise limited studies.

The following recommendations can help policymakers identify opportunities to reduce spending on redundant or ineffective programs and better address the needs of transitioning service members, veterans, and their families.

Mandate Consistent and Routine Budget Reporting for All Programs That Support Military-To-Civilian Transitions

The U.S. government should mandate increased oversight of the programs included in our study. Because the types of services that programs offer overlap, there is clearly a need for policymaker intervention to require agencies to standardize their budget and performance reporting—a mandate that should not be limited to programs that support employment transitions. The 2020 GAO report relied on self-reported budgetary data from program representatives, which introduces questions about the completeness and accuracy of this information. As we attempted to update those findings, we often found outdated and conflicting information, even for such large programs as VR&E.

Identify Opportunities to Streamline the Employment Transition Landscape and Improve Oversight

Small transition programs appear to be duplicating the efforts of the largest programs by offering similar education and employment services. Although these individual programs operate with limited budgets, they collectively receive millions of dollars in federal funding. Our review identified multiple programs that appear to serve very small numbers of beneficiaries, have not released any performance data, and might complicate the benefit process for veterans who already need to navigate an enormous number of resources. A full-scale study of small, federally funded employment transition programs would provide the necessary evidence for decisions about which programs should be shuttered or combined with other programs. Such a study would be complicated by the fact that several of these programs provide grants to other organizations that, in turn, provide services to beneficiaries.

Conduct an Independent Evaluation of the Largest Programs to Reduce Inefficiencies and Improve Performance

The vast majority of federal funding for employment transitions goes to programs that exclusively or primarily support educational opportunities. An independent evaluation of the largest programs conducted by an agency that is empowered to access detailed budget information and performance evaluation results would allow policymakers to quantify these programs' effects. Specifically, this evaluation might be designed to answer the following research question: Are *education*-focused transition programs the best investment if the goal is to help veterans obtain meaningful, well-paying civilian jobs? Although many people would answer in the affirmative, especially based on college outcomes, the evidence that supports these effects for the full population of postsecondary students is still unavailable. Further studies should explore such questions as: To what extent are these programs achieving their missions? To what extent are federal funds going toward education at the *expense* of successful employment transitions?

Refocus Military-To-Civilian Transition Support on Employment

We identified several specific directions for federal funding that could improve support for transitioning service members and veterans as they navigate the demands and opportunities of the civilian labor market:

- Federal budgets should dedicate more funding to programs that help transitioning service members, veterans, and their families immediately enter the civilian labor market and hold such programs accountable for employment outcomes. Job-placement services and programs that establish relationships with veteran-friendly employers are labor-intensive, but these individualized services can help ensure that beneficiaries do not fall through the cracks. At the same time, these programs should be systematically evaluated on the quality of their services and the extent to which they improve employment outcomes.
- The TAP is now required for most transitioning service members, and there is pressure for TAP coursework to cover a great deal of ground in a short amount of time. The TAP should renew its focus on job-finding skills, develop better skill-translator tools to help transitioning service members accurately determine which requirements they need to meet to pursue particular career paths, and provide continuing support after the service

member becomes a veteran. At the same time, veterans' preferences for their civilian occupation could differ dramatically from the occupation that they held in the military.

- Much of the funding dedicated to the PGIB is directly provided to colleges, universities, and other postsecondary training facilities through tuition payments. Policymakers should ensure that, as a condition of receiving these funds, these institutions provide adequate counseling services that are focused on veteran experiences to enrolled veterans. These services could help veterans select a course of study, link them with employers, and provide mental health and counseling services to those who need them, in addition to helping veterans navigate the federal benefits to which they might be entitled.

- There might be opportunities for DoD to outsource career counseling and to provide transitioning service members and veterans with vouchers to access the services of local private-sector professionals. These recruitment specialists might be better positioned than career counselors employed by federal agencies to help these beneficiaries transition to the civilian labor market in their local area, as well as to provide ongoing support as veterans seek to advance in their careers. However, similar to all programs that involve disbursing funding to service providers, there is a need for careful oversight and accountability for performance.

Legislative and Regulatory History of Transition Programs

Transition Programs for Veterans: Legislation and Regulatory Actions

This appendix summarizes major legislative and regulatory action regarding the largest transition programs (in terms of people or dollars): the TAP, veteran education benefits (the PGIB and MGIB), DoD's Tuition Assistance Program, VR&E, and JVSG. It is not meant as an exhaustive inventory and focuses primarily on major milestones.

TABLE A.1

The TAP and Related Initiatives

Year	Type	Name	Brief Description
1991	Legislation (Pub. L. 101-510, Section 502)	Benefits and Services for Members Being Separated or Recently Separated	Introduces TAP counseling, including information on VA benefits, programs for employment search, and financial assistance
1991	MOU	Memorandum of Understanding Between Department of Labor, Department of Defense, Department of Veterans Affairs, Transition Assistance Program Workshop And Disabled Transition Assistance Program	Establishes interagency roles to develop and smoothly execute transition assistance, as required by Pub. L. 101-510, Section 502; the ED, SBA, OPM, and DHS were added to subsequent versions
1995	Legislation (Pub. L. 103-337, Section 543)	Expansion of Personnel Adjustment, Education, and Training Programs to Include Coast Guard	Expands TAP services to the Coast Guard and makes the services available to more military members
2004	Executive order (EO 13360)	Providing Opportunities for Service-Disabled Veteran Businesses to Increase Their Federal Contracting and Subcontracting	Encourages federal contracting with disabled veteran-owned business
2009	Executive order (EO 13518)	Veterans Employment Initiative	Promotes veteran employment within the federal government

Table A.1—Continued

Year	Type	Name	Brief Description
2011	Legislation (Pub. L. 112-56, Sections 201–265)	VOW to Hire Heroes Act of 2011	Makes several changes to transition assistance, including mandating TAP counseling, individualized assessments on skill transfer, and allowing service members to apply to federal agencies using veterans' preferences prior to separation; makes changes to the Uniformed Services Employment and Reemployment Rights Act of 1994 (Pub. L. 103-353, 1994); and establishes certain limited tax credits for employing wounded warriors
2014	MOU	Transition Assistance Program for Separating Service Members	Sets forth TAP governance between VA, DOL, DoD, DHS/USCG, SBA, ED, and OPM
2015	Legislation (Pub. L. 113-291, Section 557)	Enhancement of Information Provided to Members of the Armed Forces and Veterans Regarding Use of Post-9/11 Educational Assistance and Federal Financial Aid Through Transition Assistance Program	Requires sharing more-practical information in the TAP about education benefits
2016	Regulation (Code of Federal Regulations, Title 32, Part 88)	Transition Assistance for Military Personnel	Requires identification of Career Readiness Standards and metrics to track them
2016	MOU	Transition Assistance Program for Separating Service Members	Revises 2014 MOU between VA, DOL, DoD, DHS/USCG, SBA, ED, and OPM
2018	Executive order (EO 13822)	Supporting Our Veterans During Their Transition from Uniformed Service to Civilian Life	Increases mental health care access for transitioning veterans
2018	Legislation (Pub. L. 115-407)	Veterans Benefits and Transition Act of 2018	Requires the VA to identify and publish a list of community-based programs operated by nonprofit entities that provide transition assistance to members of the armed forces who are retired, separated, or discharged
2019	Policy (DoDI 1332.35)	Transition Assistance Program (TAP) for Military Personnel	Establishes the Career Readiness Standards for the TAP

Table A.1—Continued

Year	Type	Name	Brief Description
2019	Legislation (Pub. L. 115-232, Section 552)	Improvements to Transition Assistance Program	Allows the TAP to begin one year prior to separation; requires individual counseling; establishes multiple pathways (e.g. career, education, vocational training); moves from the former three-day DOL Employment Workshop to a new mandatory one-day DOL training, which can be coupled with one or more two-day elected tracks; and requires identification of separating veterans with a high-risk of unsuccessful transition and provide them more intensive preseparation counseling
2021	Legislation (Pub. L. 116-315, Section 4305)	Johnny Isakson and David P. Roe, M.D., Veterans Health Care and Benefits Improvement Act of 2020	Requires a one-year independent assessment of the effectiveness of the TAP and a longitudinal study

NOTE: DHS = U.S. Department of Homeland Security; EO = executive order; MOU = memorandum of understand; OPM = U.S. Office of Personnel Management; USCG = U.S. Coast Guard.

TABLE A.2

Veteran Education Benefits

Year	Type	Name	Brief Description
1984	Legislation (Pub. L. 98-525, Sections 701–709)	Veterans' Educational Assistance Act of 1984	Provides educational benefits for service members who opt in with a $1,200 contribution that must be used within ten years after leaving the service; and directs preseparation counseling that consists only of counseling on educational benefits and Reserve opportunities
2008	Legislation (Pub. L. 110-252, Section 5001)	Post-9/11 Veterans Educational Assistance Act of 2008	Vastly expands veteran education assistance, including providing housing assistance and much higher tuition reimbursement, as well as allowing service members to transfer benefits to dependents
2009	Legislation (Pub. L. 111-32, Section 1002)	General Provisions	Extends benefits to (1) spouses and children of service members who died in the line of duty or from a service-connected disability while a member of the Selected Reserve and (2) reservists and National Guard members who are called to active duty for training or operations

Table A.2—Continued

Year	Type	Name	Brief Description
2011	Legislation (Pub. L. 111-377)	Post-9/11 Veterans Educational Assistance Improvements Act of 2010	Revises the PGIB, including expanding eligibility for National Guard and reservists and providing benefits for nondegree programs; and fixes the tuition reimbursement cap for private institutions at $17,500, adjusted annually based on an index of the average increase in the cost of undergraduate tuition
2013	Legislation (Pub. L. 112-239, Section 681)	Equal Treatment for Members of Coast Guard Reserve Called to Active Duty Under Title 14, United States Code	Expands eligibility for VA educational benefits to certain members of the Coast Guard Reserve
2014	Legislation (Pub. L. 113-146)	Veterans Access, Choice, and Accountability Act of 2014	Requires public universities receiving VA tuition payments to charge in-state tuition rates to qualifying beneficiaries
2015	Legislation (Pub. L. 114-92, Section 560)	Prohibition on Receipt of Unemployment Insurance While Receiving Post-9/11 Education Assistance	Prohibits veterans from receiving unemployment compensation and PGIB benefits concurrently
2017	Legislation (Pub. L. 115-48)	Harry W. Colmery Veterans Educational Assistance Act of 2017 (or Forever GI Bill)	Eliminates the requirement that education benefits be used within ten years and completed within 15 years (applicable to service members who were discharged beginning January 1, 2013); expands work-study programs; restores benefits for students affected by school closures; expands eligibility for Purple Heart recipients; and provides additional benefits for science, technology, engineering, and mathematics programs
2020	Legislation (Pub. L. 116-315, Sections 1001–1025)	Johnny Isakson and David P. Roe, M.D., Veterans Health Care and Benefits Improvement Act of 2020	Makes various adjustments to education assistance, such as requirements for in-state tuition, accreditation requirements, dependent eligibility, elimination of period of eligibility for veterans with disabilities, and assistance for veterans affected by school closures, among others

TABLE A.3
Tuition Assistance for Current Service Members

Year	Type	Name	Brief Description
1972	Legislation (Pub. L. 92-570, Section 722)	Education Expenses, Restriction	Caps tuition assistance at 75 percent of tuition and continues to require a service commitment for officers
1984	Legislation (Pub. L. 98-525, Sections 701–709)	Veterans' Educational Assistance Act of 1984	Increases the DoD tuition assistance cap to 90 percent for certain senior enlisted members
2000	Legislation (Pub. L. 106-398, Section 1602)	Modification of Authority to Pay Tuition for Off-Duty Training and Education	Removes the 75-percent cap on tuition assistance, permitting the military services to reimburse 100 percent of tuition
2004	Legislation (Pub. L. 108-375, Section 553)	Tuition Assistance for Officers	Removes some previous limitations on tuition assistance for officers, such as a service commitment
2011	Policy (DoDIs 1322.25 and 1322.19)	Voluntary Education Programs; Voluntary Education Programs in Overseas Areas	Implements regulation for DoD tuition assistance

TABLE A.4
VR&E

Year	Type	Name	Brief Description
1990	Legislation (Pub. L. 101-508, Section 8021)	Limitation of Rehabilitation Program Entitlement to Service-Disabled Veterans Rated at 20 Percent or More	Limits VR&E services to veterans with a 20-percent or higher disability rating
1996	Legislation (Pub. L. 104-275, Section 101)	Employment Handicap for Which an Individual May Receive Training and Rehabilitation Assistance	Permits VR&E for veterans with a 10-percent disability rating who have a serious employment handicap
2008	Legislation (Pub. L. 110-389, Section 334)	Longitudinal Study of Department of Veterans Affairs Vocational Rehabilitation Programs	Requires VA to conduct a 20-year longitudinal study of veterans who participated in VR&E
2011	Legislation (Pub. L. 111-377)	Post-9/11 Veterans Educational Assistance Improvements Act of 2010	Permits certain VR&E beneficiaries to receive PGIB housing benefits

TABLE A.5

JVSG

Year	Type	Name	Brief Description
1980	Legislation (Pub. L. 96-466)	Veterans' Rehabilitation and Education Amendments of 1980	Makes the basic structure of JVSG permanent rather than contingent on annual legislation
2002	Legislation (Pub. L. 107-288)	Jobs for Veterans Act	Establishes the current JVSG that is administered by DOL

Budgetary Changes to Transition Programs

We searched for budgets for veteran transition-assistance programs as a net total, not only direct personnel or administrative costs. It was difficult to find more-recent, reliable data that were as comprehensive as the data in GAO reports that reviewed 45 federally funded transition programs for service members, veterans, and dependents (GAO, 2019a; GAO, 2020). However, we were able to do so for 12 programs, as shown in Table B.1.

TABLE B.1

Updated Budget Data for Selected Programs Reviewed by GAO

Program Name	2020 GAO Budget Total ($ thousands)	2022 SAM.gov Budget Total ($ thousands)	Updated Budget Estimate ($ thousands)	Budgetary Year	Source
Enhancing Agricultural Opportunities for Military Veterans (or AgVets)	4,796		4,850	2022	GSA, 2023b
Postsecondary Education Scholarships for Veterans' Dependents (or Iraq and Afghanistan Service Grant)	337		924	2023	GSA, 2023e
Veterans Upward Bound	18,186		18,815	2021	ED, 2024
Homeless Veterans' Reintegration Program	44,930		63,000	2023	GSA, 2023c
Compensated Work Therapy	61,069		32,125	2022	VA, 2023a
DEA	553,128	1,255,511	1,177,324	2021[a]	GSA, 2023f
Personalized Career Planning and Guidance (or Chapter 36)	3,057	4,255	6,000	2021[a]	GSA, 2023h
PGIB (or Chapter 33)	11,056,959	8,134,273	11,760,672	2021[a]	GSA, 2023d
VR&E (or Chapter 31; formerly Vocational Rehabilitation and Employment)	231,472		32,000	2019	DAV, PVA, and VFW, 2019

Table B.1—Continued

Program Name	2020 GAO Budget Total ($ thousands)	2022 SAM.gov Budget Total ($ thousands)	Updated Budget Estimate ($ thousands)	Budgetary Year	Source
Warrior Training Advancement Course	934		4,700	2023	VA, 2023b
Veterans Outreach Program (or Veterans Business Outreach Center Program)	5,717		13,432	2023	GSA, 2023g
All-Volunteer Force Educational Assistance (or MGIB) – Selected Reserve	130,311	148,165	164,554	2021[a]	GSA, 2023a

SOURCES: Features 2020 GAO budget data from GAO, 2020.

NOTE: GSA = General Services Administration; DAV, PVA, and VFW = Disabled American Veterans, Paralyzed Veterans of America, and Veterans of Foreign Wars.

[a] Updated data from SAM.gov became available after this study's completion and is now listed in the column "2022 SAM.gov Budget Total."

Abbreviations

B2B	Boots to Business
COOL	Credentialing Opportunities On-Line
DEA	Survivors' and Dependents' Educational Assistance
DoD	U.S. Department of Defense
DoDI	U.S. Department of Defense Instruction
DOL	U.S. Department of Labor
ED	U.S. Department of Education
ENPP	Employment Navigator and Partnership Program
FY	fiscal year
GAO	U.S. Government Accountability Office
GSA	U.S. General Services Administration
JVSG	Jobs for Veterans State Grants
MGIB	Montgomery GI Bill
PGIB	Post-9/11 GI Bill
SBA	U.S. Small Business Administration
TAP	Transition Assistance Program
USDA	U.S. Department of Agriculture
VA	U.S. Department of Veterans Affairs
VBA	Veterans Benefits Administration
VR&E	Veteran Readiness and Employment

References

Air Force Instruction 36-2306, *Reenlistment and Extension of Enlistment in the United States Air Force*, incorporating change 1, January 27, 2021.

Army COOL—*See* Army Credentialing Opportunities On-Line.

Army Credentialing Opportunities On-Line, "Frequently Asked Questions," webpage, last updated April 2, 2024. As of April 30, 2024:
https://www.cool.osd.mil/army/costs_and_funding/index.html?FAQs

Asch, Beth J., James R. Hosek, and John T. Warner, "New Economics of Manpower in the Post–Cold War Era," in Todd Sandler and Keith Hartley, eds., *Handbook of Defense Economics: Defense in a Globalized World*, Vol. 2, Elsevier, 2007.

Barnow, Burton S., and Jeffrey Smith, *Employment and Training Programs*, National Bureau of Economic Research, Working Paper 21659, October 2015.

Barr, Andrew, Laura Kawano, Bruce Sacerdote, William Skimmyhorn, and Michael Stevens, *You Can't Handle the Truth: The Effects of the Post-9/11 GI Bill on Higher Education and Earnings*, National Bureau of Economic Research, Working Paper 29024, July 2021.

Boraas, Stephanie, Grace Roemer, and Katie Bodenlos, *Assessment of the Workforce System's Implementation of the Veterans' Priority of Service Provision of the Jobs for Veterans Act of 2002*, Mathematica Policy Research, March 2013.

Brandt, Deborah, "Drafting U.S. Literacy," *College English*, Vol. 66, No. 5, May 2004.

Collins, Benjamin, *Veterans' Benefits: The Veteran Readiness and Employment Program*, Congressional Research Service, RL34627, May 10, 2021.

Collins, Benjamin, David H. Bradley, and Katelin P. Isaacs, *Programs Available to Unemployed Workers Through the American Job Center Network*, Congressional Research Service, R43301, May 31, 2019.

Congressional Budget Office, *The Post-9/11 GI Bill: Beneficiaries, Choices, and Cost*, May 2019.

Congressional Commission on Servicemembers and Veterans Transition Assistance, *Congressional Commission on Servicemembers and Veterans Transition Assistance: Final Report*, January 14, 1999.

DAV, PVA, and VFW—*See* Disabled American Veterans, Paralyzed Veterans of America, and Veterans of Foreign Wars.

Defense Activity for Non-Traditional Education Support, "Troops to Teachers," webpage, undated. As of December 28, 2023:
https://www.dantes.mil/ttt

Department of Defense Instruction 1322.19, *Voluntary Education Programs in Overseas Areas*, incorporating change 1, April 23, 2020.

Department of Defense Instruction 1322.25, *Voluntary Education Programs*, incorporating change 4, April 2, 2020.

Disabled American Veterans, Paralyzed Veterans of America, and Veterans of Foreign Wars, *The Independent Budget for the Department of Veterans Affairs: Budget Recommendations for FY 2018 and FY 2019*, 2019.

DoDI—*See* Department of Defense Instruction.

DOL—*See* U.S. Department of Labor.

Dortch, Cassandria, *Educational Assistance Programs Administered by the U.S. Department of Veterans Affairs*, Congressional Research Service, R40723, March 15, 2011.

Dortch, Cassandria, *GI Bills Enacted Prior to 2008 and Related Veterans' Educational Assistance Programs: A Primer*, Congressional Research Service, R42785, October 6, 2017.

Dortch, Cassandria, *The Post-9/11 GI Bill: A Primer*, Congressional Research Service, R42755, updated September 23, 2021a.

Dortch, Cassandria, *Veterans' Educational Assistance Programs and Benefits: A Primer*, Congressional Research Service, R42785, updated December 3, 2021b.

Easterling, Henry Willis, Jr., *Nonmilitary Education in the United States Air Force, with Emphasis on the Period of 1945–1979*, dissertation, Indiana University, 1979.

ED—*See* U.S. Department of Education.

Fanning, Ruth, "Vocational Rehabilitation and Employment Service, Veterans Benefits Administration," testimony before the U.S. Senate Committee on Veterans' Affairs, February 5, 2008.

GAO—*See* U.S. Government Accountability Office.

GSA—*See* U.S. General Services Administration.

Kamarck, Kristy N., *Military Tuition Assistance Program: Background and Issues*, Congressional Research Service, R47875, December 14, 2023.

Kleykamp, Meredith, Gordon Rinderknecht, Shaddy Saba, Julia Vidal Verástegui, and Kayla M. Williams, *Increasing Sustainability of Veteran-Serving Employment-Focused Nonprofits: Findings from a Mixed-Methods Study*, RAND Corporation, RR-A1363-10, forthcoming.

Kofoed, Michael S., *Where Have All the GI Bill Dollars Gone? Veteran Usage and Expenditure of the Post-9/11 GI Bill*, Brookings Institution, October 2020.

Kofoed, Michael S., Lucas Gebhart, Dallas Gilmore, and Ryan Moschitto, *Zooming to Class? Experimental Evidence on College Students' Online Learning During COVID-19*, IZA—Institute of Labor Economics, Discussion Paper 14356, May 2021.

Li, Xiaoxue, "Improving the Labor Market Outcomes of US Veterans: The Long-Run Effect of the Transition Assistance Program," *Defence and Peace Economics*, Vol. 31, No. 1, 2020.

Locke, Dawn, "The Transition Assistance Program: Steps to Ensure Success for Servicemembers as They Enter Civilian Life," testimony before the U.S. House of Representatives Committee on Veterans' Affairs, Subcommittee on Economic Opportunity, May 17, 2023.

McGowan, Catherine E., *Air Force Military Tuition Assistance: A Historical Analysis*, Air War College, February 15, 2012.

Mehay, Stephen, and Elda Pema, *The Impact of the Navy's Tuition Assistance Program on the Retention and Promotion of First-Term Sailors*, Naval Postgraduate School, June 12, 2008.

Mercer, Charmaine, and Rebecca R. Skinner, *Montgomery GI Bill Education Benefits: Analysis of College Prices and Federal Student Aid Under the Higher Education Act*, Congressional Research Service, RL33281, January 19, 2007.

MyArmyBenefits, "Military OneSource," webpage, undated. As of December 28, 2023:
https://myarmybenefits.us.army.mil/Benefit-Library/Federal-Benefits/Military-OneSource-

National Park Service, "History of the National Home for Disabled Volunteer Soldiers," last updated November 14, 2017.

National Veterans' Training Institute, *Jobs for Veterans State Grants (JVSG) Primer*, updated July 2022.

O'Conner, Rosemarie, Jason Schoeneberger, and Danny Clark, *Evaluation of the Transition Assistance Program (TAP): Impact Study Report*, ICF Incorporated, LLC, July 2023.

Public Law 65-178, Vocational Rehabilitation Act, June 27, 1918.

Public Law 78-16, Rehabilitation of Veterans Disabled in Present War, March 24, 1943.

Public Law 78-346, Servicemen's Readjustment Act of 1944, June 22, 1944.

Public Law 82-550, Veterans Readjustment Assistance Act of 1952, July 16, 1952.

Public Law 84-634, War Orphans' Educational Assistance Act of 1956, June 29, 1956.

Public Law 89-358, Veterans Readjustment Benefits Act of 1966, March 3, 1966.

Public Law 92-540, Vietnam Era Veterans' Readjustment Assistance Act of 1972, October 24, 1972.

Public Law 92-570, Department of Defense Appropriation Act of 1973, October 26, 1972.

Public Law 96-466, Veterans' Rehabilitation and Education Amendments of 1980, October 17, 1980.

Public Law 98-525, Department of Defense Authorization Act of 1985, October 19, 1984.

Public Law 101-508, Omnibus Budget Reconciliation Act of 1990, November 5, 1990.

Public Law 101-510, National Defense Authorization Act for Fiscal Year 1991, November 5, 1990.

Public Law 103-353, Uniformed Services Employment and Reemployment Rights Act of 1994, October 13, 1994.

Public Law 104-275, Veterans' Benefits Improvements Act of 1996, October 9, 1996.

Public Law 106-398, Floyd D. Spence National Defense Authorization Act for Fiscal Year 2001, October 30, 2000.

Public Law 107-288, Jobs for Veterans Act, November 7, 2002.

Public Law 109-444, Veterans Programs Extension Act of 2006, December 21, 2006.

Public Law 110-252, Title V, Supplemental Appropriations Act of 2008, June 30, 2008.

Public Law 110-389, Veterans' Benefits Improvement Act of 2008, October 10, 2008.

Public Law 111-32, Supplemental Appropriations Act of 2009, June 24, 2009.

Public Law 111-377, Post-9/11 Veterans Educational Assistance Improvements Act of 2010, January 4, 2011.

Public Law 112-56, Title II, VOW to Hire Heroes Act of 2011, November 21, 2011.

Public Law 113-146, Veterans Access, Choice, and Accountability Act of 2014, August 7, 2014.

Public Law 114-92, National Defense Authorization Act for Fiscal Year 2016, November 25, 2015.

Public Law 115-48, Harry W. Colmery Veterans Educational Assistance Act of 2017, August 16, 2017.

Public Law 115-251, Department of Veterans Affairs Expiring Authorities Act of 2018, September 29, 2018.

Public Law 116-315, Johnny Isakson and David P. Roe, M.D., Veterans Health Care and Benefits Improvement Act of 2020, January 5, 2021.

Public Law 117-68, Colonel John M. McHugh Tuition Fairness for Survivors Act of 2021, November 30, 2021.

Public Law 117-328, Consolidated Appropriations Act of 2023, December 29, 2022.

Rosenberg, Linda, Mark Strayer, Stephanie Boraas, Brittany English, and Deanna Khemani, *Providing Services to Veterans Through the Public Workforce System: Descriptive Findings from the WIA Gold Standard Evaluation*, Vol. 1, Mathematica Policy Research, May 2015.

Sadacca, Robert, Janice H. Laurence, Ani S. DiFazio, H. John Rauch, and D. Wayne Hintz, *Outcome Evaluation of the Army Career and Alumni Program's Job Assistance Centers*, U.S. Army Research Institute for the Behavioral and Social Sciences, October 1995.

SBA—*See* U.S. Small Business Administration.

Schochet, Peter Z., John Burghardt, and Sheena McConnell, "Does Job Corps Work? Impact Findings from the National Job Corps Study," *American Economic Review*, Vol. 98, No. 5, December 2008.

Scott Air Force Base Military and Family Readiness Center, "Welcome to Your Transition," webpage, undated. As of January 26, 2024:
https://www.scottmfrc.com/TAP

Silva, Erin, *Participation in the Transition Assistance Program and Job Placement Outcomes of U.S. Veterans*, thesis, University of Rhode Island, 2011.

Simon, Curtis J., Sebastian Negrusa, and John T. Warner, "Educational Benefits and Military Service: An Analysis of Enlistment, Reenlistment, and Veterans' Benefit Usage 1991–2005," *Economic Inquiry*, Vol. 48, No. 4, October 2010.

Smith-Osborne, Alexa, "Does the GI Bill Support Educational Attainment for Veterans with Disabilities? Implications for Current Veterans in Resuming Civilian Life," *Journal of Sociology and Welfare*, Vol. 36, No. 4, December 2009.

Smole, David P., and Shannon S. Loane, *A Brief History of Veterans' Education Benefits and Their Value*, Congressional Research Service, RL34549, July 3, 2008.

Tennessee Department of Labor and Workforce Development, *Standard Operating Procedures: Jobs for Veterans State Grant (JVSG)*, revised May 2017.

Thompson, Shane, Natalie Hinton, Laura Hoesly, and Lauren Scott, *Veteran and Non-Veteran Job Seekers: Exploratory Analysis of Services and Outcomes for Customers of Federally-Funded Employment Services*, Summit, January 30, 2015.

Trutko, John, and Burt S. Barnow, *An Evaluation of the Priority of Service Provision of the Jobs for Veterans Act by the Workforce Investment System in Providing Services to Veterans and Other Covered Persons: Final Report*, Employment and Training Administration, U.S. Department of Labor, June 2010.

U.S. Code, Title 10, Chapter 1606, Educational Assistance for Members of the Selected Reserve.

U.S. Code, Title 38, Chapter 30, All-Volunteer Force Educational Assistance Program.

U.S. Code, Title 38, Chapter 31, Training and Rehabilitation for Veterans with Service-Connected Disabilities.

U.S. Code, Title 38, Chapter 33, Post-9/11 Educational Assistance.

U.S. Code, Title 38, Chapter 35, Survivors' and Dependents' Educational Assistance.

U.S. Code, Title 38, Chapter 41, Job Counseling, Training, and Placement Service for Veterans.

USDA—*See* U.S. Department of Agriculture.

U.S. Department of Agriculture, "Enhancing Agricultural Opportunities for Military Veterans (AgVets)," webpage, undated. As of December 28, 2023:
https://www.nifa.usda.gov/grants/programs/
enhancing-agricultural-opportunities-military-veterans-agvets

U.S. Department of Education, "Veterans Upward Bound Program: Funding Status," webpage, last updated February 1, 2024. As of April 29, 2024:
https://www2.ed.gov/programs/triovub/funding.html

U.S. Department of Labor, "About the JVSG Program," webpage, undated-a. As of December 28, 2023:
https://www.dol.gov/agencies/vets/programs/grants/state/jvsg/about

U.S. Department of Labor, "American Job Centers," webpage, undated-b. As of December 28, 2023:
https://www.dol.gov/agencies/eta/american-job-centers

U.S. Department of Labor, "Employment Navigator and Partnership Program (ENPP)," webpage, undated-c. As of January 24, 2024:
https://www.dol.gov/agencies/vets/programs/tap/employment-navigator-partnership

U.S. Department of Labor, "Jobs for Veterans State Grants (JVSG) Performance," webpage, undated-d. As of December 28, 2023:
https://www.dol.gov/agencies/vets/programs/grants/state/jvsg/performance

U.S. Department of Veterans Affairs, "VA's Vocational Rehabilitation and Employment Service Signals Transformation Through Readiness," press release, June 22, 2020.

U.S. Department of Veterans Affairs, "About VA Disability Ratings," webpage, last updated October 20, 2022. As of January 5, 2024:
https://www.va.gov/disability/about-disability-ratings/

U.S. Department of Veterans Affairs, *FY 2024 Budget Submission:* Vol. 1, *Supplemental Information and Appendices*, March 2023a.

U.S. Department of Veterans Affairs, *FY 2024 Budget Submission:* Vol. 3, *Burial and Benefits Programs and Departmental Administration*, March 2023b.

U.S. Department of Veterans Affairs, "Montgomery GI Bill Active Duty (Chapter 30) Rates," webpage, last updated September 29, 2023c. As of January 5, 2024:
https://www.va.gov/education/benefit-rates/montgomery-active-duty-rates

U.S. Department of Veterans Affairs, "Montgomery GI Bill Selected Reserve (Chapter 1606) Rates," webpage, last updated September 29, 2023d. As of January 5, 2024:
https://www.va.gov/education/benefit-rates/montgomery-selected-reserve-rates/

U.S. Department of Veterans Affairs, "Chapter 35 Rates for Survivors and Dependents," webpage, last updated October 12, 2023e. As of December 28, 2023:
https://www.va.gov/education/benefit-rates/chapter-35-rates

U.S. Department of Veterans Affairs, "VA College Toolkit: Services," webpage, last updated December 12, 2023f. As of December 28, 2023:
https://www.mentalhealth.va.gov/student-veteran/services.asp

U.S. Department of Veterans Affairs, "Post-9/11 GI Bill (Chapter 33) Rates," webpage, last updated April 22, 2024a. As of April 30, 2024:
https://www.va.gov/education/benefit-rates/post-9-11-gi-bill-rates

U.S. Department of Veterans Affairs, "Veterans Affairs Acquisition Academy (VAAA)," webpage, last updated January 18, 2024b. As of April 30, 2024:
https://www.acquisitionacademy.va.gov

U.S. General Services Administration, "All-Volunteer Force Educational Assistance," webpage, 2023a. As of January 24, 2024:
https://sam.gov/fal/d2a9ab702eab4b0ab3e2f16b6c92e35e/view

U.S. General Services Administration, "Enhancing Agricultural Opportunities for Military Veterans Competitive Grants Program," webpage, 2023b. As of January 24, 2024:
https://sam.gov/fal/ed9c996ff28a4e5dbe15b7454a9b249d/view

U.S. General Services Administration, "Homeless Veterans' Reintegration Program," webpage, 2023c. As of January 24, 2024:
https://sam.gov/fal/ef0ecec7969347a5a5dbd5a7f7e44809/view

U.S. General Services Administration, "Post-9/11 Veterans Educational Assistance," webpage, 2023d. As of January 24, 2024:
https://sam.gov/fal/54fa4d92c10d44f6bb5074f0e259826b/view

U.S. General Services Administration, "Postsecondary Education Scholarships for Veterans' Dependents," webpage, 2023e. As of January 24, 2024:
https://sam.gov/fal/b3309c2b8ff740a39f3e386d9a7c5f85/view

U.S. General Services Administration, "Survivors and Dependents Educational Assistance," webpage, 2023f. As of January 24, 2024:
https://sam.gov/fal/98b2f613afbf4c28830a201deb82efb1/view

U.S. General Services Administration, "Veterans Outreach Program," webpage, 2023g. As of January 24, 2024:
https://sam.gov/fal/3c95378b6e7b4b03a688b6ab6be375bc/view

U.S. General Services Administration, "Vocational and Educational Counseling for Servicemembers and Veterans," webpage, 2023h. As of January 24, 2024:
https://sam.gov/fal/779e468a5ca4441ca5944683d2b53905/view

U.S. Government Accountability Office, *Military Downsizing: Persons Returning to Civilian Life Need More Help from DOD*, GAO/HEHS-94-39, January 21, 1994.

U.S. Government Accountability Office, *Military and Veterans' Benefits: Enhanced Services Could Improve Transition Assistance for Reserves and National Guard*, GAO-05-544, May 20, 2005.

U.S. Government Accountability Office, *DOD Education Benefits: Increased Oversight of Tuition Assistance Programs Is Needed*, GAO-11-300, March 1, 2011.

U.S. Government Accountability Office, *Veterans' Employment and Training: Better Targeting, Coordinating, and Reporting Needed to Enhance Program Effectiveness*, GAO-13-29, December 13, 2012.

U.S. Government Accountability Office, *VA Education Benefits: VA Needs to Improve Program Management and Provide More Timely Information to Students*, GAO-13-338, May 22, 2013.

U.S. Government Accountability Office, *VA Vocational Rehabilitation and Employment: Further Program Management Improvements Are Needed*, GAO-14-363T, February 27, 2014a.

U.S. Government Accountability Office, *Transitioning Veterans: Improved Oversight Needed to Enhance Implementation of Transition Assistance Program*, GAO-14-144, March 5, 2014b.

U.S. Government Accountability Office, *DOD Education Benefits: Action Is Needed to Ensure Evaluations of Postsecondary Schools Are Useful*, GAO-14-855, September 8, 2014c.

U.S. Government Accountability Office, *Department of Defense, Office of the Secretary: Transition Assistance Program (TAP) for Military Personnel*, GAO-16-796R, July 11, 2016.

U.S. Government Accountability Office, *Transitioning Veterans: DOD Needs to Improve Performance Reporting and Monitoring for the Transition Assistance Program*, GAO-18-23, November 8, 2017.

U.S. Government Accountability Office, *Transitioning Veterans: Coast Guard Needs to Improve Data Quality and Monitoring of Its Transition Assistance Program*, GAO-18-135, April 19, 2018a.

U.S. Government Accountability Office, *VA Education Benefits: VA Needs to Ensure That It Can Continue to Provide Effective School Oversight*, GAO-19-3, November 14, 2018b.

U.S. Government Accountability Office, *Military and Veteran Support: Detailed Inventory of Federal Programs to Help Servicemembers Achieve Civilian Employment*, GAO-19-97R, January 17, 2019a.

U.S. Government Accountability Office, *DOD Education Benefits: Data on Officer Participation in and Views on Proposed Changes to the Tuition Assistance Program*, GAO-19-699R, September 16, 2019b.

U.S. Government Accountability Office, *Military and Veteran Support: Performance Goals Could Strengthen Programs That Help Servicemembers Obtain Civilian Employment*, GAO-20-416, July 9, 2020.

U.S. Government Accountability Office, *Military Personnel: DOD's Transition Assistance Program at Small or Remote Installations*, GAO-21-104608, July 21, 2021.

U.S. Government Accountability Office, *Servicemembers Transitioning to Civilian Life: DOD Can Better Leverage Performance Information to Improve Participation in Counseling Pathways*, GAO-23-104538, December 12, 2022.

U.S. Government Accountability Office, *Servicemembers Transitioning to Civilian Life: DOD Could Enhance Transition Assistance Program by Better Leveraging Performance Information*, GAO-23-106793, May 17, 2023.

U.S. Small Business Administration, "Veteran-Owned Businesses," webpage, last updated April 16, 2024a. As of April 30, 2024:
https://www.sba.gov/business-guide/grow-your-business/veteran-owned-businesses

U.S. Small Business Administration, "Veterans Business Outreach Center (VBOC) Program," webpage, last updated April 16, 2024b. As of April 30, 2024:
https://www.sba.gov/local-assistance/resource-partners/veterans-business-outreach-center-vboc-program#id-what-is-the-veterans-business-outreach-center-program

VA—*See* U.S. Department of Veterans Affairs.

VBA—*See* Veterans Benefits Administration.

Veterans Benefits Administration, *Annual Benefits Report: Fiscal Year 2018*, 2018.

Veterans Benefits Administration, *Annual Benefits Report: Fiscal Year 2022*, updated February 2023a.

Veterans Benefits Administration, "VR&E Fiscal Year 2024 Subsistence Rates," webpage, last updated September 19, 2023b. As of December 28, 2023:
https://www.benefits.va.gov/vocrehab/vrerates24.asp

Veterans Benefits Administration, "Applying for Benefits and Your Character of Discharge," webpage, last updated January 12, 2024. As of April 30, 2024:
https://www.benefits.va.gov/benefits/character_of_discharge.asp

Wenger, Jeffrey B., Ellen M. Pint, Tepring Piquado, Michael G. Shanley, Trinidad Beleche, Melissa A. Bradley, Jonathan Welch, Laura Werber, Cate Yoon, Eric J. Duckworth, and Nicole H. Curtis, *Helping Soldiers Leverage Army Knowledge, Skills, and Abilities in Civilian Jobs*, RAND Corporation, RR-1719-A, 2017. As of January 26, 2024:
https://www.rand.org/pubs/research_reports/RR1719.html

Wenger, Jeffrey B., Elizabeth Hastings Roer, and Jonathan P. Wong, *Military-to-Civilian Occupational Matching: Using the O*NET to Provide Match Recommendations for the U.S. Navy, Marine Corps, and Air Force*, RAND Corporation, RR-A2289-1, 2023. As of January 26, 2024:
https://www.rand.org/pubs/research_reports/RRA2289-1.html

Wenger, Jennie W., Trey Miller, Matthew D. Baird, Peter Buryk, Lindsay Daugherty, Marlon Graf, Simon Hollands, Salar Jahedi, and Douglas Yeung, *Are Current Military Education Benefits Efficient and Effective for the Services?* RAND Corporation, RR-1766-OSD, 2017. As of January 3, 2024:
https://www.rand.org/pubs/research_reports/RR1766.html

Wenger, Jennie W., and Jason M. Ward, *The Role of Education Benefits in Supporting Veterans as They Transition to Civilian Life*, RAND Corporation, PE-A1363-4, 2022. As of January 3, 2024:
https://www.rand.org/pubs/perspectives/PEA1363-4.html

White House, Office of Management and Budget, "Historical Tables," dataset, undated.

White House, Office of Management and Budget, "Transition Assistance Program Employment Navigator and Partnership Pilot," control number 1290-0038, February 10, 2022. As of January 24, 2024:
https://omb.report/icr/202111-1290-001

World Bank, "Armed Forces Personnel, Total—United States," dataset, 2020.